it's me, it's me, OH LORD

To Mattie Sims

God Bless You

Eunice R. Lewis

it's me, it's me, OH LORD

EUNICE RHAMES LEWIS

TATE PUBLISHING *& Enterprises*

It's Me, It's Me, Oh Lord...

This title is also available as a Tate Out Loud product. Visit www.tatepublishing.com for more information.

Published by Tate Publishing & Enterprises, LLC
127 E. Trade Center Terrace | Mustang, Oklahoma 73064 USA
1.888.361.9473 | www.tatepublishing.com

Tate Publishing is committed to excellence in the publishing industry. The company reflects the philosophy established by the founders, based on Psalm 68:11,
"The Lord gave the word and great was the company of those who published it."

Cover design by Jennifer R. Fisher
Interior design by Elizabeth A. Mason

Published in the United States of America

ISBN: 978-1-6024726-6-2
1. Christian Living: Spiritual Growth 2. Prayer/Spiritual Warfare
3. Practical Life: Personal Growth
08.01.29

Dedication

This book is dedicated to my mother who went to be with the Lord in September 1992. I thank God for allowing her to see me give my life to Him and Trusting Him for results before she went on her journey.

Acknowledgments

Thank you, Canaan Baptist Church, for encouraging me to save these letters and one day have them published.

A special thank you to Dr. Darcel Holloway for her constant encouragement and never giving up on me and the ability she saw in me to be used by God.

Foreword

I believe something magical happens when we write down our prayers. They take on life and have lasting power to heal. I also believe that our prayers are music to God's ears. As long as I have known Eunice Rhames Lewis, (nearly two decades), she has been making wonderful celestial music writing beautiful letters to God. She has generously shared theses inspiring prayers with others. Every Wednesday night at Canaan Baptist Church of Christ in Harlem, New York, I, along with countless other mid-week worshippers, anticipated hearing a new prayer that she had written. Her letters, though personal prose, moved us like a surrogate spirit speaking on our behalf.

After hearing dozens of these beautiful prayers I approached Eunice one evening and suggested that she put the prayers in a book so that even more people could read them and be blessed and empowered. I have continued to encourage her in this direction and I am delighted that this has culminated in her first book, *It's Me, It's Me Oh Lord* .

God has given Eunice many gifts which she graciously shares with all. Some of those gifts include generosity of spirit, resources, encouragement, hospitality, friendship and love. These attributes can be found in these beautiful prayers, which will inspire your soul, bless your life, encourage your heart and lift your spirit!

Reverend Dr. Darcel M. Holloway

Preface

There is no Table of Contents because these letters were not written with the intention of being published. These letters represent the how I felt when I decided to give my heart to the Lord. These letters show how my personal relationship with Him began when I felt the impulse to sit in His presence and communicate with Him. It also eventually became clear that He was developing my ability to express myself so I could have a ministry of encouraging others in a simple way, showing that everyone can be useful and has something God ordained for them, even me, who thought I had nothing to offer.

Please note there are instances where lines from various worship songs are included in my communication with the Lord; these lines just happen to come to my mind during those times, and I do not in any way take credit for those songs.

This book is published because God ordered it for His purpose.

Heavenly Father,

All these years I've been in your environment hoping that my life would one day have meaning.

Lord God, I just wanted a good family life and although I had a family of my own, it just wasn't a good life. I married twice, Lord (first marriage at age seventeen, second in my twenties), and Lord, I really tried hard to make it work; only it didn't. I just wanted what I grew up seeing on television, (in the late 50s, you know the American Dream) little did I know that it just wasn't in the plans for me.

I managed, Lord, to raise my children alone, and I thank you for sending your Angels to watch over them, allowing them to grow up unharmed. Lord, I spent so many years moving about in this life trying to survive, and I guess a lot of my decisions weren't always the right ones. I often wondered why I didn't have any visible talents that would bring me happiness; as a matter of fact I couldn't think of anything in any area that I excelled in.

Lord, I started attending the Church I grew up in more regularly (as I was always in and out in the past); this time I promise I will become more involved (joining groups and attending Bible study.) Although outwardly I don't appear shy, I'm not able to speak out about my relationship with you, I'm not sure I even have a relationship and I don't know the Bible that well. I enjoy being more involved with the church, but as I've explained on occasion, I am not a person who is comfortable speaking publicly.

So there I sat in Your House, Lord, remaining very private, and seemingly unaffected. I want to know more, I want to be able to express myself, I want to have the Spirit that I see in others, I'm crying out to you, God, that something has to happen and that I'm going to remain right there until it does.

Suddenly things began to happen, to my thinking, to my heart, incidents occurred, people came into my life with a different message, my brain that in the past contained information like a sieve, began to retain information that helped me become a new person; God decided to use me, me of all people!

God gave me words to speak, a kindness in my heart to share, compassion and sensitivity to the concerns of others, revelation of the gifts that were always there only I discarded them because I didn't recognize their importance. God's plan for my life was being revealed and He was fine-tuning it for His purpose, He gave me an abundance of love for the world to see! He gave me a way to express His goodness in the simplest way, through the sincerity of the heart...

It's me, it's me, Oh Lord, thank you for knowing and giving my life purpose.

> But God has chosen the foolish things of the world to put to shame the wise, and God has chosen the weak things of the world to put to shame the things which are mighty.
>
> (1 Corinthians 1:27)

SEPTEMBER 3, 1991

People of God

I'm before you as a messenger of the Holy Spirit to express to you the magnificent power, joy, peace, kindness and love that comes through Christ the King.

You see, a few months ago I wouldn't have been able to stand before you and utter a sound in honor of God the Almighty.

Sadly, I say I didn't have a personal relationship with our Savior; when I decided to become more involved in Canaan, the church I had been in and out of through the years, I explained on several occasions that I was uncomfortable expressing my personal feelings and also speaking publicly, thereby maintaining a very low profile.

I enjoyed going to prayer service on Wednesday night, I needed to be there.

I listened to testimony after testimony and wished that I could stand up and say something for the Lord.

There was so much in my heart, but I feared getting up before others attempting to express myself. I knew that my thoughts wouldn't come out the way I felt inside.

For such a long time I continued to go to the house of our Lord, but remained invisible.

I prayed about this and I wondered why was I left out?

I wanted God to change my life; why didn't I have any talents that could make me happy, secure and bring glory to God?

I couldn't think of anything I excelled in.

Many times I asked myself if it was possible that I didn't have the strong faith that many Christians have, as kind as I tried to be to others and with the sincere love I felt I had to offer, why was Satan steadfast on my trail?

My memory wasn't at its best, so I didn't have confidence that I could learn anything that would be meaningful at this point in my life.

On the surface I didn't portray this image of worthlessness; as a matter of fact I appeared to be just the opposite, however inside I was very insecure.

There were many things from the past I suppose if I reflect upon that attributed to this, however, I went about my life doing whatever I had to do with a smile on my face and a pleasant attitude towards others.

I was well liked by those who knew me.

Suddenly so many things began to happen to me!

I realized that I was talking to the Lord on a daily basis; situations appeared that made it clear that the Lord was with me.

My mind began to seek and retain what the Lord wanted me to know; He directed me to the greatest reference book of all times.

> I will instruct you and guide you along the best pathway for your life, I will advise you and watch your progress.
>
> (Psalm 32:8)

The kindness that was always in my heart began to really grow.

I evaluated things with more understanding and a more loving attitude.

The Lord gave me small projects to carry out and succeed in so I would gain confidence, and showed me a way to speak up in His name to those who need to hear.

I began writing on paper my conversations with our Savior, and on occasion I would share them on Wednesday night at prayer service.

Me, the person who couldn't stand up before anyone and speak up for the Lord!!

On paper I began sharing everything that was in my heart; the Lord gave me volumes of words to express the joy, happiness, and love that comes through Jesus Christ.

The Lord gave me peacefulness, allowing me to spend hours in meditation, strengthening my mind in preparation to answer His call to stay strong with His love and kindness.

> I'm leaving you with a gift, peace of mind and heart and the peace I give isn't fragile like the peace the world gives; so don't be troubled or afraid.
>
> (John 14:27)

I started counting my blessings and realized that the Lord had given me so much, only I was too blind to see!

> And by that same mighty power, he has given us all the other rich and wonderful blessings he promised; for instance, the promise to save us from the lust and rottenness all around us, and to give us his own character.
>
> (2 Peter 1:4)

Right now He's reorganizing my life, putting me on the right path, giving me a chance to be the person He wants me to be.

I can't explain how special the Lord is making me feel; I have His love and kindness in me; I'm walking with the protection of His angels watching over and caring for me.

The appreciation for all His many wonders are made known to me; every day brings knowledge of the Lord's wisdom.

I've been given the ministry of God's love and kindness to share with the world; to be an example visibly, so that all can see the glory of God; the ability to express with simplicity the glory of God; so that all can understand, to transmit sincerity, so that all can feel, the glory of God.

> God showed how much He loved us by sending His only begotten son into this wicked world so that we might have eternal life through his death.
>
> (1 John 4:9)

I thank Jesus with all my heart for bearing my sins so that I could have this chance...

What a Mighty God I serve.

July 9, 1991

Oh Mighty God,

Here I am before you, just as I am, which reveals nothing.

You, Heavenly Father, know the interior, therefore knowing that I want to move forward in your realm.

Point me in the direction that will please You, allow me to function with a broader understanding of Your word so that I can proclaim Your truth at just the right moment to those who need to hear.

Everyday, Lord, I'm aware of the presence of Your love in my life. For years I thought that I had been overlooked in terms of possessing any God-given talents, but Lord, all along You've allowed me to help many people through the years with a warm smile, kind word, encouragement and the ability to pass on a strong, positive attitude towards life, all that You've done for me has been a testimony in itself for me to share.

You've shown me how this little light can help the disenchanted.

I know You will guide me in the right direction, as a matter of fact, You're doing it right now, or these thoughts would not have come to my mind. I'm just so amazed at the way You've made me realize so much all of a sudden.

How great Thou are.

At church Mrs. Capers always tells us about her special friend, Almighty God. I now know that friend also, and the blessed assurance that comes with the friendship.

Just me, Lord

JULY 18, 1991

Oh gracious God,

I must tell You how You've come to my rescue!

I know You already know, Lord, but I've got to express myself to You. I've got to constantly tell You of my gratefulness and go over the many wonderful things that You're responsible for in my life.

Heavenly Father, I can't stop thinking about myself, and how You decided that now is the time, now is the time for me to step out in Your name!

I'm no longer Invisible, that's how I've felt; although portraying an image of sophistication by some people's standard, inside you knew that the ground work was being laid, and that my very small light that affected some would begin to illuminate to Your satisfaction.

I was to be visible in effectiveness, lobbying for the kingdom of God.

Only through Your grace is it possible for a sinner such as I can be transformed into someone bearing good news and a shining example of Your wonders.

You've blessed me all along, You've never let me down, my life experiences have supplied me with ample testimony, You've shown me that I too have something to say, and that I don't have to possess a Doctorate of

Letters Degree, You've given me volumes of words to express Your goodness, and pointed me in the direction of the greatest reference book of all, how can I not step out and speak up in the name of Jesus!

Somehow somebody's going to hear.

My way may be different, Lord God, but You've drawn out my course and navigated my destination, and I can't turn around.

Your Holy Book has become my world, I seek answers, I seek knowledge, I seek joy and fulfillment, it's all there Lord, there are no disappointments.

Loneliness, rejection, stress all disappear, Beloved Father, You've provided all that we need.

Life can have real meaning to those who know You.

You've given me all these things, Lord, and I thank You dearly for being in charge of my life and making me the person I am.

I'm astonished at the fact that things I considered of the utmost importance are no longer important; You've made me realize that very little is necessary for true happiness, and I'm no longer obsessed with possessions.

How fortunate are we who know of your special kindness.

Continue to direct my life's work, help me retain the scriptures that will encourage and direct others to your glorious kingdom.

Bless me with the endurance to be ever present with Your on-going love penetrating through to those who are unhappy.

Your faithful servant

I don't let a day go by without praising Your name.

JULY 24, 1991

Divine Father, Master of Peace and Happiness,

Here it is Wednesday again, and I feel compelled to write down my conversation with You today.

Lord God, I thank You immensely for giving this day to me, for allowing my eyes to see the wonder of Your beautiful universe, and for keeping my mind filled with thoughts of charity for others.

How I wish I could help those unfortunate souls who aren't aware of the happiness knowing You brings.

My heart has so much Love to share and I owe it all to You.

I know You have the master plan and I await Your instructions patiently.

There is so much I want to thank You for, I could go on and on, but Lord God, I'll just highlight the simple things we all take for granted.

The sun, moon, trees, birds, rivers, oh Lord, there is just so much You've given us to appreciate, I can't thank You enough.

You've given me a life filled with so many possibilities.

The list is endless for those with your joy within.

If one door is closed you open another, there are never any disappointments.

If we excel in Your Truth we know only the best life has to offer.

I can't think of anything else that offers such a guarantee that never expires.

Thank You for keeping me safe on Tuesday when a car jumped the curb while in reverse and hit a building instead of me, as I stood at the corner waiting to cross the street.

The amazement of it all was that the driver was not in the car at the time! The motor was running and when the car zoomed back and hit the building, the driver ran to the car and turned the motor off.

There I stood in direct line of danger; if the car had gone in a straight line instead of curving and hitting the building.

I can't understand how the car's gear shifted like that, I'm just so happy that You had Your angels on duty watching over and caring for me.

Twice within weeks You've shown me the protective care You provide. For so long I thought I had nothing of importance to say but You knew when You wanted me to come out in Your name.

Thank You for all that You are and all that You've made me.

JULY 31, 1991

Divine Deliverer,

I can't let a day go by without praising Your name; I must communicate the goodness I know through Your wonderful kingdom. Every day I'm inspired to speak or write of the joy I know and the many examples I see of Your everlasting harmony.

There are so many unhappy people who need to know of the peacefulness You give through the acceptance of Your son Jesus.

Satan and his demons are running wild in New York City, Lord God, and we need the strength of prayer from Your saints more than ever. I know with everything that occurs, there is a reason and only You have the answer; only through You can this havoc turn around.

I must, along with all those who know the truth, get a message through about restoring this city back into a place where people can live together harmoniously; it can only happen through acceptance of You, Lord God, as number one in our lives.

I pray all those unhappy souls will realize the power and sublime fulfillment only You provide. I'm so happy with what You've done with my life, how You've opened my eyes and stimulated my mind; I just want everyone to know the same happiness I have.

Although there is much danger and wickedness all around me, I walk in Your protective care with love in my heart.

Thank You for loving me and allowing me to know You better.

Your servant

> What's more, I am with you, and will protect you wherever you go.
>
> (Genesis 28:15)

AUGUST 8, 1991

Jesus, Jesus, everyday Your name is the same,

Yes, everyday Your name is the same, and I want Your flock to know that they can depend on You Jesus when all else fails, Jesus is there for you.

So many of us are afraid to come to You, Jesus, because we fear the change that we're expected to make once we've made a commitment to Christ. Because of ignorance of the Word we are afraid of giving up things we think are important in our lives, but how foolish some of us are.

We don't know the ultimate joy that awaits us once we allow God to take charge of our lives. Without You, Lord, there is no real happiness, and much of what we're exposed to is superficial, yet some of us are still afraid to humbly turn to You; then when disappointment and trouble overpower us, we fall on our knees and cry out to You, Lord, yet still afraid to make a complete commitment.

I ask You to deliver those in bondage and ignorant of the joy on receives in Your wonderful kingdom. I too was once afraid, but as soon as I let go and let God in, amazing changes began to happen in my life.

I've never known such peace, contentment and abundance of love that's within my soul. In you, Jesus, I have a friend with whom I can discuss and share all things as often as necessary and be sure of receiving the comfort I need.

Yes, Jesus, Jesus, everyday Your name is the same.

You've made my life so beautiful; I now look forward to each new day through a new set of eyes. I now appreciate the many wonders of Your great power in creating the universe and how blessed I am to be able to absorb it all; I ask myself how can I enhance the beauty you've so magnificently created. Thank you for giving my life beauty and quality.

There is so much we take for granted.

I realize that how much you get out of all that's available to you depends on how one views things, an example is a TV commercial that shows a glass half full or some may say the glass is half empty; the difference is a positive view or a negative one.

We're to enjoy Your kingdom with appreciation and a positive attitude, trusting You to direct our lives, and Lord, I willingly surrender mine, here I am.

Lord God, I ask You to let my mind and exterior reflect the love, security and inner peace I live in through Your protective care.

Allow the reflection of my light to shine near and far glorifying Your name and uplifting Your kingdom. I extend my thanks to You for deciding on using me Lord, as I wanted so badly to do more in Your name.

Everyday You direct me to some situation that I can be a part of in some way.

Heavenly Father, my tasks are not always big and don't call for superior intelligence, however I thank You so much for giving me an abundance of common sense and love, allowing me to communicate comfortably with those I come in contact with.

My sincere appreciation to You Lord, for always being around when I need You.

Yes Jesus, Jesus, everyday Your name is the same.

Your servant with love and trust.

AUGUST 13, 1991

My God, Holy Deliverer,

You are truly the Supreme Being; Master of all visible and invisible. I humbly stand before You in wonderment. It is not for me to question Lord, but how did you decide on me; me of all people to be a spokesperson for Your Kingdom?

Don't you remember Lord, that I am the person who in all these years found it impossible to publicly utter a sound on Your behalf, being shy about saying Your name Jesus out loud? Yet here I am almost daily with pen in hand or typing uncontrollably the amazing discoveries found in Christ.

Everyday You're giving me more insight on so many situations, and showing me how I can advance in Your kingdom while encouraging others at the same time.

My communication is from the heart Heavenly Father, very simple, yet You've shown me that to people on all levels your Word is the common denominator.

I thank You, Father, for deciding on me, because now Your vast domain is available to me.

My mind is functioning better than ever, Lord; to my surprise, I have so much to say on Your behalf, there is not enough time if I live in this world to the age of nine hundred.

I move forward in Your name.

Thank You, Lord, for deciding on me.

I'm yours, Lord, everything I am, everything I'm not;
I'm yours, Lord.

Your Servant

AUGUST 16, 1991

My Father,

I'm so concerned about sin, who of us is without it Father?

Although we walk in Your light, the perfection is not ours; Lord God, so many are afraid of not living up to Your standards. Oh Lord, we want to in every way, You've provided all the answers and helped us along the way; You've been so wonderful to those of us who know of Your unlimited love.

You've given us so much; we could never repay You in any form that would match Your generosity.

Heavenly Father, just be patient with all those as well as myself who need You and Your support system at times right here with us. We know You hate sin, Lord God, and that sin isn't measured in terms of one being greater then another, all sin is equally despised and because we love You, Lord, we want to strive towards pleasing you.

Help us in our efforts.

Keep our minds free from evil.

I'm far from perfect, but You've given me so much love and joy anyway; just because I'm Your child. The same way a parent takes away privileges, or instills a hardship in order to teach a particular lesson, to build character and strength, You've been a concerned parent all these years, doing what was best for me to learn well. I don't deserve all You've given me and I can no longer accept all Your kindness without doing something for You in return.

I will do whatever task I'm given in order to help another person, regardless of how small.

Father, the world may not be aware of my deeds, but I'm going to be on file in Your record keeping department Lord, doing whatever I can to earn recognition in my heavenly home.

I pray in the name of Jesus that You know my heart through these words; I'm not all You want me to be yet, but Father, please keep me on the path, continue to plague my mind when sin makes its attempts to ruin my joy.

It's me, it's me, it's me Oh Lord, my heart is true and I bare my soul at Your feet.

I will be the person You intended me to be.

AUGUST 26, 1991

Lord God,

Help me! Guide me in the direction of Your truth.

Lord God, I'm led by the Holy Spirit to write of my revelation; I know I can because You told me so, however Lord, there is still the fear that I'm not qualified to write such a book that all people will find something for themselves therein.

I ask You to lead me to the scriptures that will bring this book to life.

You've given me a ministry, Lord; You've shown me in so many ways that You've chosen me to stand out in Your name. I pray in the name of Jesus that You keep fear and doubt away from me. I know Your joy, I trust in You, keep me strong in Your Word, and continue to give me knowledge to build upon, so that I might be well armed to fight satan and his demons

They're trying to tear me down, but I'm trusting in You, Lord.

My weapons aren't many: love, kindness, and prayer; as a parent nurtures a child, Lord, I'm still a young child in the Word, help me to grow strong, teach me what I need to know, send those before me that know of Your strength and power.

I know few will believe the peace and love I have daily, but Lord, You gave it to me, please show me how to use this special present to lead others to the path of Your great kingdom.

August 27, 1991

Lord God, today while having lunch and reading through one of many books (*Putting Your Angels to Work* by Norvel Hayes) sent to me by my sister, my eyes fell immediately on the following; "Follow the Holy Spirit's leading; The greatest deliverance you will ever receive is deliverance from yourself."

Lord God, Thank You for giving me an answer so soon.

SEPTEMBER 4, 1991

Heavenly Father,

Why did I think being called to represent love and kindness towards others would be simple?

Simple that is to those who are not too far to the left; however, I see that many who claim God's grace still fall short on love and kindness towards others. Lord God, I myself am not perfect, and You've given me an abundance of genuine love for others.

I know that some will take kindness for stupidity, but You've helped me demonstrate Your goodness anyway, and kept me filled with gladness as proof of the joy received through acceptance of Your Son, Jesus Christ.

I'm aware that so many function daily with unkind feelings towards others, I see how some Christians segregate themselves from those they look down on, including Christians of different denominations; do they witness only to those in their own Christian environment?

I've heard Christians constantly speak of their many blessings, so often referring to material possessions, and Lord God, we should thank You for everything—for just being You, for caring. Lord, I hear You telling me that the most important thing is, *what can we say for ourselves in terms of helping the less fortunate, sharing, and showing kindness and love generally to others.*

I realize that Your love in us is the key to everything.

There isn't an area that's not covered if we function off of Your love.

It will help us bear up during the most difficult circumstances, and the most significant blessing of all will be the clean, good life in store for us under Your watchful care.

Yes, satan still roams, but with Your love and all You've equipped us with, he'll never be victorious.

What I considered a simple task has become more difficult than I imagined, however I'll be obedient to Your call and follow the guidance of the Holy Spirit; after all, You planted this seed of love in my heart, and no surgeon in all the world can remove it.

At this moment I know I'm still a long way from where You want me to be, and as time goes on I know I'll advance in knowledge of Your truth, and become more astute at accomplishing Your assignment. As I learn, God, remember I need You right now, You're showing me all that I need to do, and it's massive, Lord.

Just stay with me and show me how I'm going to effectively carry out Your will.

Lord I just keep going back to Psalm 32:8,

"I will instruct you and guide you along the best pathway for your life; I will advise you and watch your progress."

Thank You, Lord
Your Servant

September 10, 1991

Lord,

Here I am again, again, Lord; I can't stop praising Your name; Jesus, Jesus, how I love Jesus.

Thank You Lord, thank You for doing so much in my life, I can't thank You enough! I've wanted so long to know You, to have You in my life. I want to spread Your goodness through the world; I want everyone to know what happens when we give our lives to You, Lord.

I want everyone to have this joy you've given me; I want to run up to strangers and say, "Look at me! Do you see this radiance, this peacefulness of mind, this ability to love!"

> We have come to know and have believed the love which God has for us. God is love, and the one who abides in love abides in God, and God abides in him.
>
> (1 John 4:16)

Lord, I say to the lost, "Trust in the Savior!"

> Truly, truly, I say to You, he who believes in me, the works that I do shall he do also, and greater works than these shall he do; because I go to the Father.
>
> (John 14:12)

So many are existing from day to day on empty, bored, and lonely, not realizing that in Christ a whole new life begins.

> When someone becomes a Christian he becomes a brand new person inside; He is not the same anymore; a new life has begun.
>
> (2 Corinthians 5:7)

Some of us think that we have fouled up our lives so much that in order to have another chance we have to literally come out of our mothers womb and start life over, which can't happen.

Well, we can start over, we can be "Born Again," that's what the cross represents, and all we have to do is say, "Yes Lord, Yes Lord, here I am, just as I am, I'm Yours."

Thank You, Father for giving us another chance.

> Yes, all have sinned; all fall short of God's glorious ideal; yet now God declares us, "not guilty" of offending Him if we trust in Jesus Christ, who in His kindness freely takes away our sins.
>
> (Romans 3:23)

Father, somehow I'm going to help those I come in contact with know how wonderful life can be when we completely Trust in you.

Just look at me, Lord; just look at me.

Your servant

This joy that I have the world didn't give it to me, this joy that I have the world didn't give it to me, the world didn't give it and the world can't take it away.

October 7, 1991

Heavenly Father,

Please hear my humble prayer; Lord God, we at Canaan Baptist Church want to pray to You for the victory in getting our multi-purpose center built. We know that through You with prayer all things are possible. As a people in exile, I know it's time now that we pull ourselves up and move forward, it's long overdue, Lord.

It seems that too many have turned from You, Lord, and as a result the evil one have set up camp right here in our city, and we're under siege.

I'm aware that Your Word reveals its power in two ways; in destruction and in construction; we see this in Your word to Jeremiah.

If people accept your Word it will give life; if they reject your word it will bring condemnation (John3:36).

We need You Lord, please don't forsake us!

There are those of us who know the Word, want to be obedient, Lord, and put our faith and trust in You, help us step out in your name and bring back dignity and pride in our accomplishments, help us rescue our people and especially our youth from imprisonment of satan.

Give us insight to build for the future, help us understand the importance of leaving something behind Lord, so that others can benefit, and most of all, Lord, help us recognize and accept sacrifice.

I stand guilty Lord, as I know I have sacrificed for many things I've wanted in life that were insignificant, and like many others didn't consider giving much over and above that which you ask of us.

We always worry that we're going to put ourselves deep into the red. We should remember that the provision that come from You, don't come from man's system, and that we should get out of the old way and try Your way, keeping in mind that Your way is always opposite of man's principle.

> Those who sow tears shall reap joy, yes, they go out weeping, carrying seed for sowing, and return singing, carrying their sheaves.
>
> (Psalm 126:5–6)

Lord God, we're going to step out on faith, Hebrews 11 tells us, "What is Faith? It is the confident assurance that something we want is going to happen. It is the certainty that what we hope for is waiting for us, even though we cannot see it up ahead."

Your word says in Luke 11:9:, "Keep on asking and you will keep on getting, keep on looking and you will keep on finding; knock and the door will be opened."

> Therefore I say to you, all things for which you pray and ask, believe that you have received them, and they shall be granted you.
>
> (Mark 11:24)

And, Satan, we're going to tear your campsite down,
"For every child of God can obey him, defeating sin
and evil pleasure by trusting Christ to help him."
(1 John 5:4)

Thank You, Father for hearing my prayer and for helping me in my growth towards knowing You better.

Your servant

November 15, 1991

Oh Christ Lord,

Praises and honor to You forever.

You have been so wonderful to me Lord, You continue to help me grow with wisdom and knowledge, and I'm so grateful to You. I'm so happy with what You've done with me thus far.

I have done some disappointing things, Lord, and because I've fallen short, I sometimes dislike myself, and hate to come to You, because although I know how wonderful You are, and You always open Your arms to me, though I don't always deserve Your forgiveness.

> See my sorrows; feel my pain, forgive my sins.
>
> (Psalms 25:18)

> The blood of Christ who through the eternal spirit offered himself without blemish to God, cleanse your conscience from dead works to serve the Living God.
>
> (Hebrews 9:14)

So as I see the shortcomings of those around me, I also see myself; I put myself under the microscope and if it wasn't for Your grace and mercy I would be doomed.

> For Jehovah God is our light and our protector. He gives us grace and glory, no good thing will be withhold from those who walk along His Paths.
>
> (Psalm 84:11)

Everything in the three persons of the Trinity is perfect, but man and woman are not, and with all that You have provided, the divine is mixed with our personalities. So you see, Lord, when I don't measure up I'm sadden and question my strength.

> And He said unto me, My grace is sufficient for thee, for My strength is made perfect in weakness.
>
> (2 Corinthians 12:9)

The devil is using some heavy strategy with me to kill my joy and condemn me.

> Finally, be strong in the Lord and in His mighty power; put on the full armor of God so that you can take your stand against the devil's schemes.
>
> (Ephesians 6:13)

My life isn't one hundred percent right yet, and I'm depending on You to help me with it, Lord. I feel so good when I speak to others about Your Kingdom, and it gives me so much pleasure when love and kindness is felt from Your spirit through me, You are so generous and worthy to be praised.

When I'm on my praying ground I see myself under the microscope and I wonder if what You've given me is deserving? I want to be more like You, Lord, and less like the me I sometimes see under the microscope.

> And I am sure that God who began the good work within you will keep right on helping you grow in His grace until His task within you is finally finished on that day when Jesus Christ returns.
>
> (Philippians 1:6)

When You use me, Lord, to be inspirational and encouraging to others, Lord, I feel wonderfully blessed; however, I know I'll never be perfect and the growth that's taking place won't allow me to plead ignorance anymore, nor do I want to, I just hate thinking about what you went through for someone like me who's constantly praying forgiveness.

This good news tells us that God makes us ready for Heaven, makes us right in God's sight. When we put our Faith and Trust in Christ to save us, that is accomplished from start to finish by faith as the scriptures says it:

> The man who finds life will find it through trusting God.
>
> (Romans 1:17)

My hope is that You'll continue to walk with me, talk with me, and allow me to tell you all about my fears, which the evil one manifests.

Give me the fortitude to endure until You decide when.

> Call to me and I will answer you, and I will tell you great and mighty things, which you do not know.
>
> (Jeremiah 33:3)

Yes, ask anything using my name and I will do it.
(John 14:4)

Thank You so much, Lord, for hearing me and for providing answers for me right away.

Your grateful servant

Have a little talk with Jesus, tell Him all about your troubles.

DECEMBER 3, 1991

Oh Most Holy Father,

I once again want to talk to You and ask You a few things.

First, I Thank You for all You've done with me, and I can't stop thinking about how You're opening my eyes and mind to see and evaluate all that You bring before me.

I'm constantly amazed at how You're preparing me to walk in Your wonderful light. Lord, I thank You; I thank You for making me aware of what real happiness is all about.

Most of us fear change, we see Christians as representative of a lifestyle that's dull and boring. Praise You, Lord, when we're in Your covenant a new wonderful life begins.

"Oh, put God to the test and see how kind He is! See for yourself the ways His mercies shower down on all who Trust in Him. If you belong to the Lord, reverence Him, for everyone who does this has everything He needs."

Lord, I started this conversation saying that I wanted to ask You a few things, but as I talk of Your goodness,

I'm so overwhelmed with joy that anything else that was on my mind will have to wait until another time.

Lord, I have everything I need.

All Praises To You!

DECEMBER 31, 1991

Supreme One, The One and Only True Living God,

My Father, as this year comes to an end I praise, honor, and glorify Your name. Thank You for Your son Jesus Christ and for new life, which began early spring of this year. It has been so wonderful this year Father; I just thank You for so many blessings!!

> I will sing Your praises, I will try to walk a blameless path, but now I need Your help, especially in my home, where I long to act as I should.
>
> (Psalm 101:1, 2)

Mostly I thank You for wisdom, knowledge, love and daily growth.

Thank You for providing me with everything I need. Thank You for allowing me to be discerning enough to know that which is not of You, but that of the evil one. Help me to remain strong and able to protect Your good work. I pray Lord for those still in darkness and who know not the joy You provide. It's so difficult to understand how some refuse to try Your way in spite of continued failure or outward success with inward emptiness.

Thank You again Father for leading me toward a clean life and a loving attitude.

Father I see You directing me towards a prayer life, interceding for those unfortunate, burdened souls in the world, as well as those who are undergoing pain in various areas, as You test their faith and trust, preparing them to walk in Your light reflecting Your will.

We Christians understand the scripture:

> Weeping may endure for a night, but joy cometh in the morning.
>
> (Psalm 30:5)

If it is Your will that I know the power of prayer, then I know You will teach me all I need to know and baptize me with the power necessary.

Lord, right now I'm so weak in that area, but more than anything I want to be strong in praying for others, please help me!

I trust that in Your time I'll be representative of Your plan whatever it is.

I just agonize over the misery all around me.

Father please explain to me how I can feel such joy and happiness and bring encouragement to others; and then in my quiet times agonize over the pain of others so deeply?

Right now Lord I'm trying to find a balance for my ministry.

Since You claimed me Lord, so much has happened.

I just Thank You for giving my life real purpose.

I pray the same for those I love.

> It was through what His Son did that God cleared a path for everything to come to Him; all things in heaven and on the earth; for Christ's death on the cross has made peace with God for all by His blood. This includes you who were once so far away from God. You were His enemies, hated Him, and were separated from Him by your evil thoughts and actions, yet now He has brought you back as His friends. He has done this through the death on the cross of His own human body, and now as a result Christ has brought you into the very presence of God, and you are standing there before Him with nothing left against you.
>
> (Colossians 1: 20, 22)

Thank You Jesus!

Precious Father, Lord of Lords,

Again I humbly come into Your presence writing words from my heart to You; All honor and praise to you, and I thank You for all that You've done in my life and Your faithfulness in spite of the many times I've let You down.

I ask that You penetrate the hearts of those who are unable to physically care for themselves anymore, as the years have had its toil on them, and are now in nursing homes.

Praise You, Lord, You've upheld them in so many ways, but because of the changes in their lives from the familiarity of their home life to the unfamiliar surrounding, new faces and adjustments that aren't easy for them; they often feel lost and forgotten.

Many of their family members and friends have left them behind to be in that heavenly place You've prepared.

The enemy continue his attempts in making them fearful and insecure; some of the sadness I see during my visits often saddens me, and leaves me wanting to do something that will help strengthen their hope; there are many reasons why they aren't as grounded in the Word as they should be. This doesn't apply to all, but so many Lord, so many.

My heartache for those who feel forsaken.

> Fear not, for I am with you, be not dismayed, for I am your God. I will strengthen you, yes, I will help you. I will uphold you with My righteous hand."
>
> (Isaiah 41:10)

I pray that You help remind them that there is power in prayer and that prayer is something that can be done whatever the circumstances. We know that anxiousness is not the right reaction to have during difficult times; prayer and thanksgiving should prevail.

Your word says in Philippians 4:6, 7:

> Be careful for nothing, but in everything by prayer and supplication with thanksgiving let your request be made known unto God. And the peace of God which passeth all understanding shall keep your hearts and minds through Christ Jesus.

I ask that peace be given unto them Lord.

As Your servant Paul endured prison, but was still a witness for You Lord, enable those who know You, to remember with joy and be a witness to those in their presence, as there are many who belong to the evil one, and those who just never seek Your face.

I pray Lord that You embrace them with Your love and keep their mind at peace.

Your servant

January 19, 1992

Father God,

Thank you so much for the wonderful victory, Lord, I'm so happy with the wonderful way in which you demonstrate Your loving-kindness.

I don't deserve all You're doing for me Lord.

I'm trying so hard to make myself approved, however, I continue to fall short in many areas.

> He is merciful and tender toward those who don't deserve it; He is slow to get angry, and full of kindness and love. He never bears a grudge, nor remains angry forever. He has not punished us as we deserve for all our sins, for His mercy toward those who fear and honor Him is as great as the height of the heavens above the earth.
>
> (Psalm 103:8, 12)

My mind is absorbed in learning Your ways, I seek knowledge in every area, I pray the way the spirit directs me, I praise Your name in all the many ways, I revel in Your glory, and bask in Your gentle mercies.

I'll never be good enough, but I'll never stop trying.

Everyday you reveal so much to me.

Thank you for giving me a discerning spirit so I can know where Your presence exists and where it doesn't.

Thank You, Lord, for all the spiritual beings that You've brought before me to help keep my soul filled with the fullness of You.

Glory to You, Father, Son and Holy Spirit.

Lord, there are so many concerns in my heart, but I can't change my thoughts from the joyousness within my spirit for this most glorious week You've given me.

I just want to praise You in my entire atmosphere with my whole heart, and yes, Lord, yes, Lord, to Your will.

I'll tell the world, and thank You for showing me how to be satisfied in an unsatisfying world.

> Do you want to be truly rich? You already are if you are happy and good.
>
> (1 Timothy 6:6)

Your servant

January 20, 1992

Oh Wonderful Lord,

I'm at home on this Martin Luther King, Jr., Birthday observation.

I'm listening to songs of praise and glory to You Lord, and my mind is occupied completely in Your realm. I'm reminded of all the beauty that You expose Your people to; the beauty that's felt deep in the soul Lord.

I'm so joyous as I think of the talents You've given us and how wonderful it is when we use these talents to lift up Your program.

I'm hearing new instrumental compositions by young talents, all in the name of Jesus; My ears hear preachers with extraordinary methods in making an impact with the Word of God, and I'm here in the midst of it all, filled with the spirit of Your love and appreciation for it all.

Thank You so much for allowing me to be a part of Your kingdom. How I wish every soul knew Your joy and that their hope comes from you.

> Let all the joys of the Godly well up in praise to the Lord, for it is right to praise Him. Play joyous melodies of praise upon the lyre and on the harp.

> Compose new songs of praise to Him, accompanied skillfully on the harp, sing joyfully.
>
> (Psalm 33:1, 3)

Your servant

With all of my heart, I'm going to praise His name, with all of my heart.

March 16, 1992

Father God,

All praises and honor I give to You; Thank You so much for all Your blessings.

Monday satan gave the attack command using his most powerful demon spirits in an attempt to prevent me from going to the Holy Land with Canaan Baptist Church and receiving special blessings from You, Lord.

As a result of satan's command, my sister suffered a heart attack the day before I was to leave and was hospitalized. I cried out to You Lord to please help me and not let anything prevent me from going to the place where You walked.

Praise Your name my sister's condition was stabilized, easing my mind, but in satan's desperation, he tripled his demon force and three hours before I was to leave on Tuesday, I fell on my foot and broke a bone; at that moment I felt the presence of despair and frustration. I just started praying for Your help, and everyone at the hospital began working to get me out of there in time to make my flight since I was determined to still go. Instead of putting a cast on my foot, they put a thick wrap on it (soft cast), gave me crutches, and sent me on my way, saying they would put a hard cast on when I returned.

Praise you Lord when I called Canaan Church at the exact hour we were to leave, Rev. Walker said I could still go; I know his decision was through You, Lord, I Thank You so much.

I kept my mind focused on Calvary, surely if You could endure what You did for me, I was willing to deal with the discomfort of one broken bone.

I knew You wanted me there.

As I clumsily moved about trying to get my bags and think of what I might have forgotten, I felt satan's evil spirits everywhere in an all out attack. I couldn't think, I was overcome by nervousness, anxiety and couldn't control the flood of tears; I just pleaded with You, Lord, to help me get out of there!

Glory to You, Your angelic force just lifted me up, put me in a cab and took me on my way, got me to the airport on time, and stayed with me throughout the trip, allowing me to move about with the help of the saints from the church, seeing all You wanted me to see—blessing me with knowledge to witness to others with sincere love, kindness, and truth You've given me. Your Word says:

> Don't be afraid; Speak out! Don't quit for I am with you and no one can harm you.
>
> (Acts 18:9, 10)

Your servant, with deep appreciation for allowing me this trip at this time in my spiritual growth

March 27, 1992

8:45 a.m.

Heavenly Father,

Thank You so much for this day! I'm so excited Lord because less than a half hour ago I was able to pray in the spirit, Thank You so much for this gift, I've wanted to for so long.

God stay with me, help me to be more like You want me to be.

I want to spread the Word about Your kingdom, I want to effectively help those who are troubled by telling of Your goodness.

Help me Holy Ghost, help me.

Give me the power I need, not for prestige, but for your glorification Lord, so all can see how powerful You are.

I honor, praise and just lift up Your Holy name, without You I know nothing is possible. My faith lies with You, I believe Your Word.

> For by one spirit are we all baptized into one body.
>
> (1 Corinthians 12:13)

Thank you for answering my prayers.

> If you abide in me, and my words abide in you, ask whatever you wish, and it will be done for you.
>
> (John 15:7)

Help me Lord, help me.

APRIL 13, 1992

Lord God,

I cry out to You, please continue Your good work within me.

Your Word promises in Philippians 1:6:

> For I am confident of this very thing, that He who began a good work in you will perfect it until the day of Christ Jesus.

Lord God I believe that.

So many things are trying to cause me to backslide, and Lord I'm fighting it and remembering what Your word promises, You've given me all power, why is this happening?

I'm trying so hard to listen and not make a mistake Lord.

Unsaved people are pulling me down, even so called Christians! Just being in their environment, hearing comments unbecoming of Christians, and Lord sometimes I tend to fall short myself.

When I'm alone at home my heart tells me how ungodly it all is, and I'm saddened because I'm allowing this to happen, Lord please help me!

Lord I need my privacy, I need to be alone with You

for a while, I need to build myself up and I know how to do it.

Why are these obstacles before me? Is there a purpose or is the enemy riding my back?

Reveal to me the truth Lord; reveal to me Your plan.

My spirit tells me that my ministry can be more powerful although it seems so simple.

Show me Lord what I need to know.

So much is happening to me and I don't want to misinterpret anything.

> As it is written in the scripture, this shall all be taught of God. Those the Father speaks to, who learn the truth from Him will be attracted to me.
>
> (John 6:45)

I sit at Your feet Your willing servant.

April 24, 1992

Lord God,

There's going to be a revival at our church, our faith reinforced, our commitment strengthened. The word of God convicting every unsaved soul

> The good news tells us that God makes us ready for heaven, makes us right in God's sight, when we put our faith and trust in Christ to save us. This is accomplished from start to finish by faith. As the scriptures says it, "The man who finds life will find it through trusting God."
>
> (Romans 1:17)

Lord Jesus there are those at Canaan Church who stand strong on Your word, and work diligently at kingdom building, praising Your name Heavenly father, thanking You everyday for all the great things You do.

The enemy attempts to wear us down but we are prepared with the sword of the Spirit.

We claim the victory and are steadfast with Your truth.

We thank You Father for providing us with people who bring to us additional strength through the power of the Holy Spirit to fill our souls.

For those who don't know You Lord, I ask that You continue to provide examples for them to see how hopeless everything is without You as first in their lives.

I pray for their deliverance.

Lord Jesus we claim the victory for a mighty revival, for we are Your servants, we know that You supply all our needs.

> For we are His workmanship, created in Christ Jesus for good works which God prepared beforehand, that we should walk in them.
>
> (Ephesians 2:10)

We're here tonight demonstrating our devotion to You Lord; lifting up and glorifying Your name first and depending on You. We don't doubt You Lord, not for one minute. We know that if we believe in You, our God we will have success.

Glory to Your Holy Name!

Lord we're going to be here tonight in prayer and praise, believing You for a freshening in our spirit, because we want to be as effective as we can be in doing Your work here on earth.

Your servant

> And we will never forsake You again, revive us to trust in You.
>
> (Psalm 80:18)

June 15, 1992

Father God I stand in awe of You, I stand, I stand in awe of You, all Praise to You. You are the King of Kings, Lord of Lords, and You Reign in Majesty.

Lord,

You confirm to me everything I'm ever in doubt about in presenting what I feel in my heart; Your presence is always there. I must share with You and Your people an experience I had on Monday night as I see a message in it.

Monday night I attended a seminar on public speaking in the courtroom for lawyers, and in the boardroom for corporate persons, or all others that speak publicly. In any case I decided to attend because I've not overcome my nervousness in speaking publicly and thought I could benefit from this class, or at least learn some breathing techniques.

I thought about it and wondered if I really should attend such a class, since most of what I generally attempt to express is spiritual, and I feel the presence of the Holy Spirit who I trust to teach me and guide me, but I was still led to this class.

Everyone had to prepare a short speech and bring with them to demonstrate how they project and are perceived.

I didn't know exactly what I could write since everything I write is of God and this group I knew was a mixture of many nationalities and as it turned out, many attorneys.

I wanted to write something that was non-sectarian but still reflect God's plan.

I prepared my so-called speech which the Lord put in my heart and it all lined up with Your Word, God, although I never used the word God or made any religious reference outright.

I was the last to speak and after my speech everyone sat there looking convicted, there was no criticism as was with the others, and the instructor said she felt like saying a great Amen when I was finished!

My theme was about demonstrating love, kindness and concern for our fellowman, mentioning some of the ugliness that is evident everywhere.

Praise you, Lord, that is the main theme of Your Word, and it was felt by everyone there.

You further confirmed it on Tuesday when Rev. Jesse Jackson's speech at the Democratic convention touched on the same theme as mine; his was more powerful, but said much of the same thing, A man of such credentials, plus people at the seminar with all kinds of titles behind their names, and me, Lord, with my newly acquired title from the most Supreme of all the Universe—Eunice Rhames, BA (Born Again).

Your title Lord gives me confidence to sit among

titles of all descriptions comfortably, because my BA status has qualified me to recognize that it's only what one does in line with Your Word that counts.

Lord I stand; I stand in awe of You and the many wonders You provide for Your people.

I'm not a five-talent servant, or even a two, but I thank You for what might be just one Lord.

It's in my heart, which You know and I use for Your Glory,

I'm just so happy that my Lord reigns!
Let the earth Rejoice!
I stand in awe of You.
Lord I bring unto You my gratitude,
I come by the blood of the Lamb,
And I minister unto You.
Your servant

> I am the Lord Your God, and none else, and my people shall never be ashamed.
>
> (Joel 14:23)

MAY 16, 1994

Oh Father!

Here we are in Your house, laying our concerns at Your feet, and asking to hear from You. There are so many problems and situations that need Your intervention. There is incomprehensible turmoil all over the world, wickedness of every description, false prophets, idolatry, disobedience, and lack of sincere love and kindness, even among those who claim You as their own.

We come to pray for revival, revival of our spirit to love and care, for life-giving spirit, whose power is ours through Christ Jesus; I'm standing on Your Word in prayer for a great revival of our hearts and the hearts of people all over the world. Your Word says, "Come unto me all yea who are weary and heavy laden and I will give You rest," many feel unworthy, and focus on their weakness, instead of on Your strength because of guilt, but the blood of Jesus has made it possible for us to come boldly to the throne of grace and receive mercy and grace to help during the time of trouble.

I'm believing Your Word to go forth and not return to You empty (Isaiah 55:11). We need you, we need strength to walk this Christian walk; there are those who are trying so hard, without any recognition in the natural, there are those who don't say much, there are those who say everything right in Your house, and still allow the enemy to use them. I pray for all to operate in the spirit and receive all Your kingdom provides.

Guide us to growth and maturity so we can carry the Gospel boldly to all corners of the earth. Help us to encourage the brokenhearted, to distinguish and encourage those who are seeking to know more of You; help us to be recognized as people of God; speak to us through all the many ways, speak to us and fill us with the fuel we need at our upcoming revival. Let revival start with each of us individually—touch the depth of our souls so that we can be a blessing to those we come in contact with.

We all need You Lord, don't let us become full of ourselves, help us to be careful of the viciousness of the tongue, to realize the importance of a smile, give us a sensitive heart, free from envy; You've given us all something special, help us to unite together in unity so that all the gifts can work together for kingdom building.

It's so sad that the world with all its technology and scientific knowledge prefer trusting satan and as a result we see what's happening.

There's so much we have to pray about, so much.

Father in the name of Jesus, help us and those that are lost!

Help those realize that You are the one who holds the solution.

Help those realize that You are a Wonderful Counselor.

Help those realize that You are a friend like no other.

Help those realize that You make the impossible, possible.

Help those realize that You give life purpose.

Help those realize that You give Joy that the world can't give and the world can't take away.

Lord I depend on You, Your promises and the Love You provide for me.

Your servant

October 5, 1994

I'm disturbed by the low spirit many Christians are feeling right now, and this does not leave me out Lord, as I experience the same feelings at times; however, I want to cry out to You. I want to lay my heart at your feet, and ask for strengthening for myself and all the other saints who need Your power to revive.

Sometimes we feel low because we don't have the life we want at home, or maybe at work; we're insecure or unhappy, and even in our church many times we feel the enemy's presence.

Our children disappoint us, unfulfilling relationships exist, or we're just plain bored and lonely.

Sometimes we even have to force ourselves to fast and pray!

We are so imperfect Lord and need Your help all the way, Your Word says the Christians life is not an easy one. Our struggle is not against flesh and blood, but against power of this dark world, spiritual forces.

We should endure hardships with the joy of doing it for Christ Jesus.

The enemy is everywhere we go, we have to be strong in the Faith, Your Word is true, God's people all over the world suffer for Christ, but Victory is ours through Jesus

Christ. If we're not grounded in Christ, satan can easily steal our joy, but we should remember he is a liar and the father of lies, there is no truth in him. He often masquerades as an angel of light in order to deceive the people of God, we must know the enemy and how he operates.

Matthew 22:7 says:

> Thou shalt love the Lord thy God with all they heart and with all thy soul, and with all thy mind.

If we love You Lord with all our heart, soul and mind, plus love our neighbor as ourselves, not only will we be truly pleasing to You, but our spirit will be high and lifted up, enabling us to do that which is of You with joy in our heart; and the ability to wait on You for the plan You have for our lives, understanding and wisdom will be grated to us in order for us to see beyond the surface of situations.

Things of the world compete with our devotion to You Lord, we must keep our focus on You, we must not forget Your promises, we must reflect on how good You've been to us and how You've brought us through so many times.

When everything is going well we find it so easy to rejoice in You, but as soon as the going gets tough we're so easy to forget, but that's the time we should remember who You are and how great you are. When we are weak, You are made strong; You are the Truth, the Way, and the Life.

You've supplied us with all we need; we're equipped for victory, with the belt of truth, which is knowing Your Word; the breastplate of righteousness, which is living a clean life; our feet fitted with readiness from the Gospel of peace, which is carrying into all corners of the world, preaching the Gospel of Jesus Christ; the shield of faith, which is faith grounded not open to deception; the helmet of salvation, which is confidence over the fear of death; sword of the Spirit, Word of God, which is a guideline and protection against evil; and prayer, which is staying close to you Lord (Ephesians 6:14).

I say to the people of God to rejoice, rejoice, give praise, praise is for us, it opens the door for You to enter and create in us the right spirit for miracles to happen.

The Lord will make a way when there seems to be no way, He's the great I am, the Lord is good, a refuge in times of trouble, who cares for those who trust in Him.

He is our hiding place, and will protect us from trouble and surround us with songs of deliverance.

Though You have made me see troubles, many and bitter, You will restore my life again; from the depths of the earth You will bring me up.

You are the Way, the Truth and the Life.

Love him with all your heart, soul, and mind.

Seek first the kingdom of God and all other things will be granted unto you.

His word will not return to you void, aren't we a witness.

> Do not gloat over me, my enemy! Though I have fallen, I will rise. Though I sit in darkness, the Lord will be my light. Because I have sinned against him, I will bear the Lord's wrath, until he pleads my case

and established my right. He will bring me out into the light; I will see his righteousness.

(Micah 7:8, 9)

I have told you this so that my joy may be in You and that your joy may be complete.

(John 15:11)

Thank You Father for hearing my plea and for lifting my spirit with Your answer.

Your servant

June 9, 1995

Father, Father,

Speak to my heart; speak to my heart about this warm gentle spirit, whom I knew for just a short moment in time. We were drawn together and exchanged good Christian conversation from time to time, mostly on the telephone; I needed someone of her caliber to talk to.

Although she offered to share her hospitality to me at her home, for some reason I just didn't get there; why didn't I act faster?

I didn't get to taste the meal she wanted to prepare, nor share the thoughts she might have had, or just be in her home enjoying the company of a good Christian woman. It would have meant to much to me, I could have learned from her knowledge and wisdom and I just didn't get there in time.

So much is beyond my understanding, why she briefly passed my way, only God knows. I think there's a message for me since more than once I didn't get there in time.

Father speak to my heart and reveal to me Your purpose, speak to my heart and direct my path.

Thank You so much for the short time we knew each other, for the sensitivity I feel towards her spirit, for taking her home in such a quick, peaceful journey, Lord she saw

> A new heaven and a new earth, for the first heaven and the first earth had passed away, and there was no longer any sea, she saw the Holy City, the new Jerusalem, coming down out of heaven from God, prepared as a bride beautifully dressed for her husband, and she heard a loud voice from the throne saying, "Now the dwelling of God is with men, and he will live with them. They will be his people, and God himself will be with them and be their God. He will wipe every tear from their eyes. There will be no more death or mourning or crying or pain, for the old order of things has passed away."
>
> (Revelation 21:1–4)

Lord I will try to never procrastinate again when I know there is something I need to do.

NOVEMBER 14, 1995

Oh Father,

Why is there so much hatred all over the world? Why can't love be the main focal point? Why don't we make a serious effort to at least try?

Everywhere in all areas of life, hatred prevails; even in Your house there's evidence of the evil one's presence.

My heart grieves for all those whose lives are empty and meaningless, or lost in death cause by senseless hatred.

We must come to You Father, on our knees, praying for Your guidance in helping us love the way You want us to, not the way we do it, on today, off tomorrow! Judging others unfairly, cruel comments, ungodly conversation, unwilling spirit in helping others in their efforts to glorify You and their attempts to grow in Christ.

Why Lord why?

You've given us authority over evil; You've provided all we need. How did so many of Your people become so comfortable in part-time Christianity? If we're committed to Your way, studying Your word, meditating and praying, why aren't we loving, sharing, and caring?

So much is superficial.

Oh Lord, I feel Your presence in my heart; I want the

world to know of Your great plan. The plan that comes from the wonderful Prince of peace, the plan that restores dignity, the plan that provides all one needs according to Your riches in glory, the plan that provides a shield in the time of trouble to those who trust You, the plan that puts joy in our heart that the world can't take away. We know with Your plan tears may last all night, but in the morning there is joy; with Your plan there is no room for hate, we don't see skin color, we just recognize all those who are walking in love and anointed by the Holy One. Our hearts equally overflow; we worship in unity and peace, praising and honoring the one and only living God. In Your plan we are not anxious, we let our requests be made known to You, through prayer, supplication and thanksgiving. In Your plan we shall not want, for You guard, feed, and care for us. In Your plan we do good to those who hate us, and bless them that curse us.

In Your plan we pray for those who despitefully use us; in Your plan we render to no man evil for evil. In Your plan we can do all things through You Christ who strengthens us. In Your plan we can come boldly to the throne of grace and obtain mercy and find grace to help us in the time of need. In Your plan we are never forsaken, in Your plan we don't have a spirit of fear, but of power, love, and a sound mind.

Thank You Father, oh thank You Lord, in Your plan we have assurance of answered prayer. Thanks be to You who gives us the victory! Therefore I say, submit to God, resist the devil and he will flee from you; there is power in His Blood, victory comes in His name, by His Word.

I don't worry, because everything is in His hand, I

can sing a victory song, I don't worry about the government and their policies, I can sing a victory song in the worst of times, I don't worry about the mysteries of the world, they belong to You God, I can sing a victory song because the battle is Yours.

If we are in Christ then who can be against us and win for greater is he that is in us then he who is in the world, I sing unto you a victory song.

Hallelujah!

DECEMBER 2, 1995

If anybody asks you, where I'm going, where I'm going soon. I'm going up yonder, I'm going up yonder, I'm going up yonder to be with my Lord, As God gives me grace, I'm running this race, until I see my savior face to face. I'm going up yonder, going up yonder yes I am.

Thank You, Lord, for granting me desire to see my children grow up to be adults without physical harm done to them. Lord, this prayer I've carried for what seems like such a long time, but I can say to You, I see how faithful You are. Lord, I've done many things through the years that I'm not proud of, and you could have forsaken me rightfully so, but You didn't, because the most important desire of my heart You granted. My children are now young adults and the foundation has been laid, the rest is in Your plan.

I thank You for getting them to this point; when I start my journey up yonder to be with You, Lord, my soul will be at peace, because I was there while they were young and needed me most, now it's their turn to make decisions for their lives.

There are so many things I have to be grateful for because You have been so good to me, You also allowed me to spend some of the most precious moments one could hope for with my mother before she began her journey up yonder to be with You.

I thank You so much for all that You put in my heart for her to see, because it made her so happy to know that You were actively working in my life, it was probably her prayers for our entire family that You answered and allowed her to leave us rejoicing, because the last time I saw her face, she was lying there smiling, I'll never forget what You've done for me Lord, I'll never forget.

Thank You for directing me to Your Word for guidance, your Word as my source, Your Word for strength, Your Word for comfort. Thank You for accepting me as an heir to Your kingdom and all I've inherited, the many promises I can stand on.

Promises of salvation, promises of spiritual growth, promises for my personal needs; for times of loneliness, fear, anger, frustration, suffering, discouragement, trouble, sickness, temptation, sadness, bereavement, and for a home up yonder with You in everlasting glory!

> How precious also are Your thoughts to me, O God!
> How great is the sum of them.
>
> (Psalm 139:17)

I wholeheartedly meditate on Your Word, because I know all is inspired by You God—all—and that the writers wrote what was breathed out by You; You spoke through them, giving all a chance to live in this world victoriously during a period of approximately 2000 years, written in three languages (Hebrew, Aramaic, Greek) with one great theme and central figure, Jesus Christ! Who could be responsible, none other than the Supreme Author, the Holy Spirit of you God,

The God of the past, present and future,
The God who holds everything in His Hand,
The God who sits high and looks low,
The God who offers hope in a world of
hopelessness.
Because in the beginning God created the Heavens and the Earth and said, Let there be...
Let there be; in your Word "Let there be" was said eight times, thus the heaven and the earth were made complete in all their vast array in six days, resting and blessing the seventh.
The God who holds everything in His hand...
The God who rescued you and me...
The God who gave us all a story to tell, a love to share, a life to live...

So if anyone asks you, where I'm going, where I'm going soon, tell them for me, I'm going up yonder, I'm going up yonder to be with my Lord, yes I am, oh yes I am...

January 2, 1996

> And these signs will accompany those who believe In My name they will drive out demons, they will speak in other tongues they will pick up snakes with their hands and when they drink deadly poison it will not hurt them at all; they will place their hands on sick people, and they will get well.
>
> (Mark 16:16, 18)

Abba Father,

Although I've been in prayer to You all through the night, I have to bring my petition boldly before You and the saints of Canaan, because I need prayer for my brother who has been admitted to the hospital. He's been sick and taking tests for the last three to four weeks and the result from the biopsy show that he has a tumor on his liver. Right now he's being built up since in the last few weeks he has been unable to eat, thereby losing weight. His system is weak, so after he's built up, he will undergo treatment or surgery.

Father, I believe in You and miracles, I know You are the miracle worker, You said if I have faith as small as a mustard seed, that is enough, but my faith far exceeds the size of a mustard seed and I'm believing in You for healing of my brother. I thank You for bringing me to a place where I can accept whatever You decide, but Lord, until the last breath is breathed, I won't give up hope, I'll carry Your word in my heart, that as a child of God I have authority over sickness, so I pray for my brother, I'll lay hands on him Father as I pray and repeat Mark 16:18.

I'll remember the days of Hezekiah sick unto death, and the prophet Isaiah, Hezekiah turning his face to the wall, praying,

> I beseech thee, O Lord, remember now, How I have walked before thee in truth and with a perfect heart, and have done that which is good in thy sight, and Hezekiah wept very much and it came to pass before Isaiah was gone out into the middle court that the word of the Lord came to him saying, return and tell Hezekiah the captain of My people thus saith the Lord the God of David, thy Father, I have heard thy prayer, I have seen thy tears, behold I will heal thee, On the third day thou shalt go up unto the house of the Lord and I will add unto thy days fifteen years.
>
> (2 Kings 20: 1–6)

Father as Your child, I will not give up yet, I claim him as part of my household, I will pray, I will exercise the authority You've given for healing, I will cry out day and night, I will seek the payers of the saints until the last breath is breathed, I will have hope because like Hezekiah, maybe You'll hear and spare my brother.

Your word says "Let us hold fast the confessions of

our hope without wavering, for He who promised is faithful" (Hebrews 10:23).

I stand on Your promises and thank You for the victory.

> But He was wounded for our transgressions, He was bruised for our iniquities; the chastisement of our peace was upon Him; and with His stripes we are healed.
>
> (Isaiah 53:5)

AUGUST 13, 1996

Oh Most Holy Father,

Many of our people are living in defeat; they're living in defeat because the enemy (devil) has captured them, and has a stronghold on their lives. Father many of them are so tired, so tired of living in such a hell, so tired of feeling the despair, hopelessness, and level of disrespect the enemy has them earning everyday of their lives; Because they are so down and out, how can they think for a moment that You or anyone loves them? Some have committed such lowly crimes that they can't even love themselves; they feel helpless against the powers of the one who comes to steal, destroy and kill, but, Father, I am here to plead to You for them. Your Word says, those that the Father has given me no one shall snatch them from you, that we can expect You to answer our prayers, so, Lord, I come to You in prayer. I'm asking that You reveal to them the assurance of salvation, that You did not send Your son into the world to condemn the world, but that the world through Him might be saved (John 3:17). I'm here hoping that they'll see through all those who are here today extending Your love and kindness that they can become a part of the family, the family of Jesus Christ.

We can all connect and become one with You Christ and that through You we inherit riches and knowledge unmatched by anything known here on earth... We become a new creation, the old goes away and the new makes its debut...

We receive wisdom above that of man... Your Word says to:

> Trust in the Lord with all your heart and lean not on your own understanding; In all your ways acknowledge him, and he will make your path straight.
>
> (Proverbs 3:5, 6)

Father I don't understand everything, nor do I need to, I leave the mysteries to You, I can just demonstrate to the world by my example what happens when we sincerely love and trust You with our life.

We can be the best that we can be; because of You, everyone here can live a victorious life and become an admiral in Your army against the wiles of the enemy, after all Lord, who has better experience and knowledge of the deceitful, cunning strategies of the evil one then those imprisoned? They can help so many others, thereby using their past to do good, working for the King.

All our hope comes from You, help those living in defeat realize that they can live in victory, and that it's not too late.

> As for God, His way is perfect; the Word of the Lord is proven, He is a shield to all who trust in Him.
>
> (Psalm 18:50)

He'll make a way out of no way, all power is in His hands, He'll give you a life and life more abundantly, Oh what a friend we have in Jesus, we just have to carry everything to Him in prayer...

I'm so glad that You care for us, Lord, I'm so glad that we can come to Your feet; I'm so glad that through all our trials and circumstances we can depend on You to be there with us all the way. I'm so glad that no temptation can overcome us except that which is common to man, but You are faithful and will not allow us to be tempted beyond what we are able; but with temptation you will also make a way of escape, that we will be able to bear it. I'm so glad that when we are at our lowest point, when we belong to You, You will uphold us with Your righteous right hand. I'm so glad that as our provider I don't have to worry about food, shelter, or my body being clothed; I can rely on You to keep my mind at peace and joy in my heart through the worst of times. Oh, Lord, help Your children, don't let them fall by the side of the road, and those that are down, give them the strength to pull themselves up, enter their minds with power and knowledge of the one and only true living God.

I thank You, Lord, for being my God, for being the same yesterday, today, and tomorrow. I thank You for being my all and all, I thank You for knowing all our needs, for there is something each of us have a need of, and we thank You for being the God who cares for us; we thank You for every day that we open our eyes and see a brand new day; we thank You for giving us a chance to choose life or death, even when we didn't deserve it. Thank You, Lord, for giving us hope, thank You, Lord, for giving us an opportunity to be broken, and discouraged; at that point you embrace us, equip us with the sword of the Spirit, which is your Word, and we rise, we rise victoriously, strong conquerors, walking tall, loving and helping each other as children of God, because we are one, one in the Spirit, covered by Your blood, Hallelujah! Praise God we're one.

Thank You Lord for allowing me this moment to speak with You and gather with all that are here, please help us bridge the gap, Your grace is sufficient. And because Your strength is made perfect in weakness, we know that in our weakness You are strong.

> Ask and it will be given to you, seek and you will find, knock and the door will be opened to you, For everyone who asks receives; he who seeks finds; and to him who knocks the door will be opened.
>
> (Matthew 7:7)

March 10, 1998

Lord Jesus,

I don't know what Your divine plan is for this life of mine, but I'm Yours, use me for Your purpose; mold me, shape me to Your satisfaction, guide my steps, give me Your wisdom and understanding to help build Your kingdom here on earth. So often I agonize over whether I'm at the place I should be in order to successfully carry out the plan You have for me, but I know that whatever You plan for Your saints you'll also prepare them, and that we should fear not because You didn't give us a spirit of fear but of love, power, and a sound mind.

The enemy continues to try everything to hold me in bondage, but Lord I've come too far and know too much about who You are, what You're capable of, and that those who the Father has given you no one shall snatch them away. I can do all things through Christ who strengthens me, the flesh will not defeat me, nor will the enemy have his way.

I stand on all that the Holy Spirit has put in my heart and when I begin to doubt myself Lord, help bring me back to the place where you first showed me Your great love and power.

I thank You Lord over and over again, there is so

much I owe You for giving my life meaning, for allowing me to be a part of Your wonderful kingdom and inheriting all that goes with it.

Thank You Lord for life, thank You Lord for my daily bread, thank You Lord for shelter, and the comfort of a home where I can comfortably meditate on Your Word, pray and fill my space with joyous music praising Your precious name. Thank You so much Lord for the growth You have allowed me through so many different sources, I just can't thank You enough, there are so many things in nature one takes for granted, but Lord I will never forget who made everything possible, who created heaven and earth, who first loved me and gave me the right to eternal life, oh thank You, Lord, thank You.

As I retire to a night's rest my mind will be on You Lord, and when I awake in the morning light, I'll awake singing praises to Your name.

May 6, 1998

Father God,

Tonight I stand to uplift and glorify Your name, Lord, I give You all the honor; Oh how sweet the sound, Jesus the name about all others, all power is in Your hand, and how grateful I am for that, Father.

Everyday the enemy moves about seeking to steal, destroy, and kill, but Hallelujah! I'm so happy that he has no win with me. I'm so happy because I've studied to make myself approved, I'm so happy because I know that I know that I know; no weapon formed against a child of God shall prosper, I know that for those who serve You can expect good things to manifest.

I know when I'm down and discouraged, You'll send someone with a message from You that will put me right back where I belong, because You'll never leave or forsake Your own. Your word says that those that the Father has given you no one can snatch them away. I know that the possibilities for growth, knowledge, wisdom, love, and favor are limitless, because You want Your disciples to be a light for all the world to see and know how great You are. Our God, the God who erased all fear of death, through his son, Jesus Christ, and made it possible to have everlasting life reigns over all the earth with majesty, glory, and unlimited power holds the entire world in His Hands.

Hallelujah! Hallelujah!! Glory and honor to the One and only true living God.

May 31, 1998

> I will bless the Lord at all times His praise shall continually be in my mouth. My soul shall make her boast in the Lord, the humble shall hear of it, and be glad, Oh Magnify the Lord with me.
>
> (Psalm 34:1, 3)

I thank You, I thank You for the privilege of honoring You, for the privilege to call Your name, for the privilege of being able to come into Your presence and give You all the praise. The privilege of carrying You in my heart, the heart You gave me. How incomprehensible it is, the depth of Your love for Your children, but Father, I'm so grateful for it and feel so special because of it.

Your love has opened up a whole new world for me, and my efforts to walk in that love has made a real person out of me; giving me something to say, a kind spirit to share, and heartfelt concern and compassion for those You put in my path. Oh Yes, Lord, here I am, use me!

Use me for Your glory, use me to stir-up the spirit in others; You put Your spirit in all of us, and if we just allow ourselves to be still and let You do Your thing with our lives, we can be all that You want us to be without stress and strain.

We can all sparkle in our own special way when we listen to You and stop trying so hard to please and impress man. Father, for so many years I thought all I had was a personality, but we all have a personality. Thank you, Lord, for letting us keep our individual personalities, because our personality teamed up with Your Godly direction allows us to reach all the many different types that comprise this world. So thank You for the privilege of being me, for those who are affected in a positive way by my personality. You are so wise Lord, You show us that for everything there is a reason.

I continually lift You up because Lord, Your blood has made me whole; and although my understanding is not the same as Yours. Thank You for giving me, even me, the capacity to know what I know and let it show, so that You will be glorified.

By some standards I may not appear to do much, and by my own evaluation, I should do more; I guess that's because I'm aware of what You've done in my life and the ministry You've given me to encourage others. I Thank You for all that You've done, You've given me all that I need for success by Your standards, Help me to stay focused on the path You paved for me, so as I function in this life, I strive to do more for You because Lord, the love I carry in my heart, and the suffering I witness everyday by those who don't know You, make me think about doing more. There must be more I can do.

Thank You for giving me a reason for being here and giving me a song to sing in the best and worst of times, it is my most honored privilege to serve and magnify Your name, Your name above all others, God the Father, Son, and Holy Spirit. Amen, amen.

June 10, 1998

Lord Jesus,

Just when we think we can relax and bask in Your presence, the devil drops by and attempts to have his say. My calm has been disturbed, and suddenly I'm surrounded with stress and burdened with a truckload of financial obligations, that were unexpected. Father God, I don't feel good always appealing to You for financial help. I know that You're the only one that can fix any situation, but Lord, I hate having one problem after another; at this moment Lord, this is the way I feel.

You've given me so much and made me realize it, because for so many years I thought I was left out and had nothing to offer. I've had so much growth in Your kingdom, and Lord I thank You so much for that.

I know as an heir to Your kingdom, I can claim victory in every area; the devil can't win. While he's frantically trying to tear me down, Your Word is fast in building me up—life and power is in the Word of God. No weapon formed against me shall prosper, the Lord is my defender and I will never be defeated. Yes, I'm bold and strong, I banish fear and doubt! I know the Lord my God is with me wherever I go, the Lord will make a way for those who love Him. I've never seen the righteous forsaken, I can tell You my troubles for You are my refuge,

I can move mountains by just having faith even as small as a mustard seed, Oh thank You Jesus! Thank You for knowing me, down to every hair on my head, now isn't that good news?

The devil's attacks can't harm me; I'm fully equipped with the sword of the spirit. Weeping may last for a night, but in the morning there is joy, hallelujah! Thank You Lord, even though I walk through the valley of the shadow of death I will fear no evil for You are with me; Your rod and staff, they comfort me. You prepare a table before me in the presence of my enemies. You anoint my head with oil; my cup overflows. Surely goodness and love will follow me all the days of my life, and I will dwell in the house of the lord forever (Psalm 23).

What a mighty God I serve, what a mighty God I serve,
Angels bow before Him, Heaven and Earth adore Him,
what a Mighty God I serve.

My problems are over; my God will supply my needs.

JULY 7, 1998

Dearest Father,

I have a dream, Lord, I have a dream that is clearly seen, and deeply felt in my heart.

I want to represent a godly woman, Lord; a godly woman who clearly is blessed by You; who is given a ministry of encouragement that is anointed and serves Your purpose in kingdom building. I want to gather women together and let the ministry You gave me move something in their spirit that will help them here on earth. Lord everything that I have, everything that is made known to me, every move that I make, let it glorify You, Lord.

I realize, Father, that I have a long way to go in my growth, and I ask desperately for Your help in the many areas. I'm so far from where I want to be Lord, and only You can help me. I can't do it without Your intervention.

Please help smooth out the rough edges! Please let more of You show and less of me!

Give me the full understanding of my ministry; I want to sparkle for You, Lord; allow my ministry to draw those You choose; let me represent a new wave for You; plant my feet on solid ground and use me, use me, Lord.

Let the Holy Ghost take control as I magnify You Lord, shine on me, let Your Holy Ghost power shine on me.

I am a child of the King, I come from royal stock, I'm a joint heir with Jesus Christ; I've inherited the riches of Christ, and I'm seated with Him in heavenly places. I lift up my head and sing.

My Father is rich in houses and lands,
He holdeth the wealth of the world in His hands!
Of rubies and diamonds, of silver and gold,
His coffers are full, He has riches untold

Chorus

I am a child of the King, a child of the King;
With Jesus my Savior, I'm a child of the King!
I once was an outcast stranger on earth,
A sinner by choice and an alien by birth,
But I've been adopted, my name's written down,
An heir to a mansion, a robe, and a crown.

(from *Too Blessed To Be Stressed*,
Dr. Suzan D. Johnson Cook)

I'm Yours Lord, Use me.

JULY 9, 1998

Abba Father,

I know that I don't have to continually put my son before You Lord, because You have already heard my plea, so many times, but every time I come across something in Your word that speaks to my heart and assures me of Your promises, I just have to bring it before You. This is for me and for all the mothers who are praying for sons that have gone astray. We know that we have made mistakes along the way, but Lord, we did what we knew and much of what we knew was influenced by things of the world. For that I ask Your forgiveness—for not paying attention to all the many things and ways You were trying to get my attention.

Since I decided to put You first in my life so much is coming together for me, and I'm so indebted to You. Here I am Lord, I'm Yours.

For my son and all the sons who mothers are praying for, Your word says:

> Thus says the Lord: A voice was heard in Ramah, lamentation and bitter weeping, Rachel weeping for her children, refusing to be comforted for her children, Because they are no more. Thus says the Lord: refrain your voice from weeping, and your

eyes from tears; For your work shall be rewarded, says the Lord. And they shall come back from the land of the enemy. There is hope in your future, says the Lord, that your children shall come back to their own border.

(Jeremiah 31:15–17)

But the mercy of the Lord is from everlasting to everlasting on those who fear Him, and His righteousness to children's children.

(Psalm 103:17)

You shall also know that your descendants shall be many, and your offspring like the grass of the earth. You shall come to the grave at a full age, as a sheaf of grain ripens in its season. Behold, this we have search out; It is true, Hear it and know for yourself.

(Job 5: 25, 27)

I know that You are true to Your word, so I again stand on it for my son and the sons of other praying women; You will do Your part and I will do mine. I'll work for You, Lord, and my compensation/benefits package includes my family, Thank You Jesus!

Thank You for accepting me as I am and giving me a chance to become what You want me to be. Thank You for never being too weary to listen to me and providing me with all I need to live life in the comfort of Your love.

Your servant,
Eunice

Can a woman forget her nursing child, and not have compassion on the son of her womb? Surly they may forget, yet I will not forget you.

(Isaiah 49:15)

July 10, 1998

Father God,

At this moment I am on vacation, and I thank You for my job, and the vacation I've been allowed. I've had a wonderful few days away in the south attending a few reunions. It was good to be away, enjoying the company of friends and those I met doing that time. I still have a few days left to my vacation time and I intend to do a few things in the nature of house cleaning, but mostly, Lord, I want to relax with my mind on You. I'm so thankful for all You've done in my life and I just want to reflect on that, Lord.

I want to sing; I want to rejoice, because You are so deserving of all honor and glory. Praise Your precious name, Jesus!

What would I do without You in my life, how would I manage through all the evil that surrounds me, day by day? I am so blessed to be able to come to You with all my concerns, and be fully persuaded, wavering not, because I know You Lord—You never fail us, You're always there and if I want to talk with You, You make yourself available in so many ways. You're talking with now as I write this letter, or better yet as I open your Word, there You are in every page I turn, revealing to me all that I need to know to be victorious through every situation; hallelujah, praise You, Father!

This love that You give is so overflowing my spirit can't contain it all. I look around and my eyes are full of the beauty of Your creation. Here I am with all that I need and more Lord. Thank You, Jesus!

I thank You, Lord for being here right now in the Laundromat, as I wash my household belongings, how many are there in other parts of the world who don't have the facilities, or funds to wash clothes the way I can.

My apartment right now needs a good cleaning Lord, thank You for the apartment, thank You for all the food that's in my refrigerator, (I have too much, Lord—look at me I need to lose weight!) bring some before me to share all that You've given me, I'm Yours Lord, just use me, however You decide.

I want to be a better servant, help me, and convict me at every twist and turn, when I'm out of Your divine order. My clothes are finished now, Lord, but as I leave this place, my heart is full of love for You and my fellow man.

July 17, 1998

Lord God,

I am just so in awe of You, You are God all by yourself. There is nothing that is impossible for You; how great You are! In this world there is so much hurt and pain; everyday we are faced with one disappointment after another. We see our youth milling about hopelessly; we see disrespect and dishonor forced on women all over the world; we see men and women led by the enemy; living shameless lives; abusing themselves, their children and disrespecting You, Lord. Those attempting to live a godly life, struggling because of the overwhelming attacks of the devil—it seems to require so much to just survive.

But, I'm convinced that there is help, there is victory in spite of all the gloom. When we turn to You, Lord, when we dare to remember who You are, when we just look toward heaven, we can have hope; we can grieve for the world and still be in peace. We can go about doing Your work and have joy in our heart. We can relax in Your comfort, we can count on You as our guide; when we are weak, You demonstrate Your strength. You are God almighty—the God of mercy and grace, the God of righteousness and justification! You are the God of deliverance, abundant life and love.

You are God almighty! The maker of the universe, who put the stars in the sky, the sun and the moon; I just look around and observe Your greatness, how amazingly awesome! You are God Almighty! How majestic is Your name. The name is Jesus, and I call on you in the best and worst of times, times of fear, loneliness, anger, frustration, guilt, suffering, discouragement, temptation, sickness, bereavement, need, and You always come forth, because You're a blessing to those who seek You. You are God Almighty!

Your promises are true: for my family, finance, and for victory over satan. You've overcome the things of the world, satan is a loser! You are God Almighty, my God will reign forever!

You are faithful, and will guard me from the evil one. Sin will not have dominion over me—You have delivered me from the power of darkness and transferred me into the kingdom of righteousness. You are God Almighty! Blessed are those who seek You.

> Those who are planted in the house of the Lord shall flourish in the courts of our God.
>
> (Psalm 92:13)

Thank You for Your love, and I pray for Your love to grow in me more and more everyday.

Your servant

Father God,

It's me; it's me Lord,

Here I am, over here seeking the presence of Your company. I need to talk, I need to confirm what I know through Your Word, I need to be strengthened by it, I need to be comforted and feel the warmth of Your love, I need to praise, worship, and give reverence to Your holy name. I lift Your name up as the one and only true living God. I confess that I am not all yet that You intended me to be, but everyday I attempt in some way to be a blessing to You, and that You forgive my shortcomings and continue to help me fulfill my destiny.

Lord God, Your Word says that in Christ we become a new creature, it's right here:

> Therefore if any man/woman be in Christ he is a new creation; old things have passed away, behold all things have become new.
>
> (2 Corinthians 5:17)

And Lord, I thank You for that. I know You Lord; I believe You to be who You say You are, and can do what You say You can do, Your Word is alive! Your Word is manna from heaven, and my thirst is quenched with living water, You're the author and finisher of my faith, I am in Christ and called by Your name.

Father, I am a woman of virtue, I am in Christ, I am in covenant with You, I have the anointed one living in me, I have the power to trample serpents in the name of Jesus, I am an overcomer with the authority to use Your name, no foul spirit can conquer me, because I am more than a conqueror, I am in Christ!

Your promises are true and I can claim them, I am an heir to Your Kingdom and entitled to all Your benefits. I am not intimidated by the world's ungodly standards or man's puffed up nature, I come from a royal priesthood, I am in Christ, my needs are supplied over and above.

You said there will be times of trouble, but You will never leave or forsake me because trouble may endure for a night but in the morning there is joy.

There is no situation that will destroy me; my trust has been transferred from me to You. I believe in the resurrected Christ as Lord and Savior, I am Your child, I am in Christ, my mind is renewed; I am Your righteousness, my heart is filled with Your love, Even when I fall short, Your spirit won't let me be contended, You help me correct my wrongs immediately, and always give me another chance, I can't be comfortable in sin, I want to be pleasing to You, I want the world to see You in me, I want to be that light in places of darkness.

I will not be separated from You; You have been faithful to me, You have looked deep into my heart, You know my concerns, You know my passions.

I see Your hand in every area of my life, I see my dreams realized, the windows of heaven have opened and blessings are overflowing, I don't walk in fear because I am in Christ and nothing is impossible for me.

I am a woman of faith, a woman who has taken the time to know You, know what Your word says, and know its benefits for my family, relationships, finance, future, health, and purpose for my life. Everyday You open my mind to more knowledge of You; I'm not perfect and still there's much more to learn, but in my imperfections You demonstrate Your strength. I am in Christ, I proudly share Your presence in my life, I witness and encourage wherever You give me opportunity. Eternal life is mine, heaven is my home; thank You Lord for that Wonderful gift, I am forever grateful.

In the midst of disaster I can claim the victory; I'm fully equipped. I'm the daughter of Eve, created in the image of You, God, filled with Your spirit and walking in Your love.

You just keeping doing great things for me. You have truly smiled in me—yes You've been good to me. I'm so glad I found a Savior, and He's sweet I know. Jesus, Jesus, wonderful Jesus, You are Savior, You are Lord, and You are God, and just to be close to You is my desire.

My Father, my Lord, my God,

As I open my eyes to a brand new day, I take a deep breath and just give honor, glory and thanksgiving to You for allowing me to be here and able to face whatever challenges I may face on this day. I don't anticipate any problems, but instead look forward to being a blessing to someone in whatever small way that I can.

I am equipped to handle anything the devil might have in mind to spoil my day; it just won't happen because Your spirit dwells in me and I intend to be recognized as one of Your disciples by the fruit that I bear.

You've been so good to me and everyday I'm amazed at the growth that has taken place as I study to make myself approved. I may not be all that I should be yet, but You have brought me a mighty long way from where I started.

I depend on You, Lord, and I have not feared, because You did not give me a spirit of fear, but of power, love, and a strong mind, and even at my lowest point, I can still have joy. You see, I believe Your Word to be true so I stand on all Your promises, and know that as I delight myself in You, You will grant me the desires of my heart. I see that happening everyday, and if You never did I will love You anyway because in my trusting You I know You look out for my best interest, and Your understanding is higher than mine. This I know: You are with me always, Your Word says:

> For the lord your God is a merciful God. He will not forsake you nor destroy you, nor forget the covenant of your fathers which He swore to them.
>
> (Deuteronomy 4:31)

As a spiritual descendant of Abraham by faith in Jesus, I'm an heir in the Kingdom of God and with that comes all the blessings and promises which will give me success in all areas. This I carry in my heart, soul, and spirit so through hard times, adverse situations, sickness, death, and disappointment from others, I walk in victory because Lord, You and I are the tag team that wins.

> Let your conversation be without covetousness; and be content with such things as ye have; for He hath said, I will never leave thee, nor forsake thee.
>
> (Hebrews 13:5)

July 11, 1998

Father,

It's now 3:00 a.m. and I'm preparing to go to bed now, but I just wanted to speak with You for a moment. I want You to know that I'm filled with gratitude to You for Your faithfulness and for giving me something to strengthen my faith. I needed to see an obvious move from You on my behalf, Lord, and You provided that for me through my son. I'm just so filled with joy and I thank You so much for it.

Today I reflect on all the many wonders of You, Lord, and Your beautiful universe. I appreciate these days you've given me to just relax and devote my time to You—it's been so refreshing. My mind is calm and I just want to readjust my schedule in order to fit in comfortably all the things I want to do for Kingdom building that will glorify You. There is so much that needs to be done; my heart rejoices when I hear of the good works done by other saints, and I feel I'm not doing enough.

Direct my path and show me signs that I'm doing right, Lord.

I just never feel worthy of so much love from You when I know how imperfect I am.

You give so much and I feel I never give enough,

but Lord, I will do better and I sure am better than I ever was, thanks to You, and I know You're not finished with me yet. Your word says that this good work that You began in me will be completed and that You will keep on guiding me all my life with Your wisdom and counsel. I believe You, Lord; I believe You.

Good night, I'll talk to you tomorrow, Love You.

Your servant.

July 15, 1998

Father,

I will not go to bed with a heavy heart for You have answered me in Psalm 27:5–6. I am not meant to be defeated by the enemy, because greater is he that is in me than he that is in the world. I am a walking testimony of Your spirit in me, so before I retire this night I will sing a song of praise and honor to the God of all that is good and perfect. Who loved me even when I didn't love myself.

Everyday is a day of thanksgiving
God's been so good to me
Everyday He's blessing me
Everyday is a day of thanksgiving
Take the time and glorify the Lord today
He keeps on blessing me.
Praise Him, praise Him, praise Him
Jesus, blessed savior, He's worthy to be praised
Glory, glory in all things give Him glory
Jesus blessed savior; He's worthy to be praised
From the rising of the sun, until the going down
of the same
He's worthy to be praised

Thanks be to You, Lord, for restoring my sprit and allowing me to go to bed with songs of praise in my heart and assurance of answered prayers.

Your servant

AUGUST 3, 1998

Father it's me,

Where do we go when we are hurting, hurting really bad?

When in our hearts the grief that's there just can't be alleviated. So many situations exist... Where do we go, how do we get relief, the bitterness, the unforgiveness, the fear? We all at some time or another undergo some of these feelings. Are we ever prepared, maybe not, so what do we do when some of these bad things invade our space? How do we find peace during such an unpeaceful time in which we live? Everybody seems to be out of control! How can we restore harmony among people, where is the overall concern, why is there so much energy spent on doing harm rather than good? Why is everything simple made difficult?

Conversation is deplorable, rather than respectful or kind, even when the elderly are present. How can one feel other than depressed and discouraged?

Your word has been removed from the schools and replaced with drugs, alcohol, sex, weapons, fear, and murder. Morality among adults seemingly non-existent to the point where they are viewed by youth as hypocrites on all levels. How can the few who are truly trying to be an example be effective when they are out numbered by the massive representatives of evil? And even they are struggling day by day to stay on the straight and narrow.

It is just so hard sometime when the saved and unsaved are all here together and there are more of them then us; Yes Lord, we know the answer; we know that Your word is true, and that if Your people who are called by Your name will turn from their evil ways, seek Your face and pray, then will You look to heaven and heal the land. O yes, Lord, we know the answer is with You, we know that when we continue to hear the word our faith is renewed, and when we are discouraged You will put someone in our presence that will uplift our spirit. Yes, Lord, we know who reigns supreme in all the earth and in Your time all will be taken care of, we just have to wear the full armor and remember the war is not ours, but yours Lord.

In our attempt to be effective for You Christ we don't give up and we let our testimony speak for us.

AUGUST 12, 1998

Father God,

Today was another day filled with thoughts of You and all Your many blessings; it's so good to be in the knowledge of who You are. I think about all that time I spent not aware and all the time I wasted, but because of Your grace and mercy here I am being used for Your glory! All my mistakes in life You made use of in my witness to others, You gave me words to speak that are of Your wisdom, me the one who, on my own can't verbalize well or remember important facts. I am a true example of what You can do.

I'm filled with gratitude and give You all the honor for molding me into the person I am now. Lord, I just want all those who are not walking in Your divine plan for their life to understand that all it takes is faith, trust, obedience, dedication to Your Word and love. If one is sincere in letting You take control, everything else will follow. There are so many unhappy people and they don't want to believe that You, Lord, are the answer.

Father, continue to help me with my ministry, help me to see clearly what it is You want me to do, help me to be better at organizing my time and to accomplish that which is important. I don't have it all together yet, but I want to, Lord, I want to.

You've given me so much to work with and I am truly appreciative, I've come a mighty long way from where I was, I just want to be all that You want me to be, I just want to walk in Your light and be a blessing to You.

So I ask for Your continued support, Your continued love, and all that I may need from You to help someone along the way.

AUGUST 20, 1998

Here I am, Lord, here I am,

I pray for Your guidance, I pray for Your faithfulness through all my short comings, I pray for strength in my attempt to be the person You want me to be; Lord it's not easy, we think that all that is involved is to love You and everything else will fall in place, but as much as I want to walk upright in Your sight, I fail, Yes Lord, I fail.

I need Your help; I so desperately need Your help. I think of how You've sustained me with Your mercy and grace, where would I be without Your loving kindness, where would I be.

Help me to be a blessing to You; let me not forget for a moment all the things You've brought me through. You've given me knowledge and understanding that has opened up a whole new world for me—the Kingdom of God—and even I can feel special in Your sight; confidence in areas that in the past were strongholds; praise the name of Jesus!

You were always there for me at my lowest moments You reign supreme and reminded me who You are.

Yes here I am Lord, here I am, feeling weak, but the devil is a liar, I can do all things through You who strengthen me.

Let me never forget.

Father God,

It is 3:15 p.m.; August 29, 1998 I am high in the sky among the clouds, flying home from a beautiful vacation in St. Martin; thank You again for affording me this time to relax my mind and body. I have been functioning at such a fast pace and really needed some quiet time. I'm grateful that my long time friend Michele and I were able to travel together after so many years, thirty-five years of friendship to be exact.

I'm so happy that we both know You and that we both are traveling on the path that You prepared as best we can. My prayers have been that those I've loved through the years would know the greatness of Your reign and allow You to direct their growth. So, Lord, I thank You for working wonders in my household, but also among friendships that I've acquired and have attachments to.

I've had such a peaceful time this week and I can only glorify and praise my father in heaven for it. I'm thinking about all the many memories of places and people I've come to know; I'm thinking of my mother and thanking You for giving me many fond events that we shared and the memorial I'm fortunate to have as keepsakes that will pass through generations of our family here on earth.

Yes Father, this week was really special, so special to me, You opened my eyes to many things, and it was so obvious how much I've changed. No longer do I have to depend on others or be influenced by the events around me, even when there is actually nothing wrong going on, but it's just about being the new me, being able to just relax in Your surrounding and that being enough.

Hallelujah praise the lamb, hallelujah!

Use me for Your purpose, mold me and make me the person You intended me to be, help me with all the rough edges so that You will be glorified. I don't know all the answers to life's mysteries, that's for You, You are God, and I'm just Your servant, just give me what I need to do Your service.

God You are the light of my life, You promise to keep me, never to leave me and You've never come short of Your word, You are my all and all.

August 31, 1998

Father God,

Here I am in St. Martin, such a beautiful island in the Caribbean, another area of Your creation. As I sit in awe of its beauty, I just thank You for allowing me the privilege of enjoying this serene peacefulness at this moment in my life. I have so much to be thankful for; I so needed this time to rest and relax my body and mind. This is such a wonderful reward.

As I move about among people of this island I pray for unity, I pray that people attempt to love each other the way You loved us. We are one; one in the spirit and if we could spread that love from one end of the earth to the other, how much better life would be.

I'm here, Lord, because of Your kind generosity, I'm here because You know my need of a peaceful environment, I came to You and You fulfilled my request, everyday for this time spent on this island I will glorify Your great name, Jesus.

I will never forget from where my blessings come and even when I can't see the purpose of all the many events that occur I will trust You because Your understanding is different from mine and Your plans always work.

Please help me to walk this walk the way You would

have me to and if I fall from time to time pick me up and place me back on solid ground.

Thank You for all You're dong for me, my family and friends.

September 19, 1998

Lord Jesus,

I thank You for this day, this day especially because I feel I've done the thing I think You wanted most and that's to take the gospel into all the world; evangelizing, encouraging the disenchanted.

Today I concentrated on that command and put it into action, going into a shelter, and hotel for the disadvantaged, plus street ministry, oh lord what a fulfilling day You provided for me! My heart was filled with such joy.

Joy because I was doing Your will, Thank You, Lord, for using me! Using me for Your purpose. You made my day so complete, after the shelter, resident hotel, and street witness, I spent one hour in the gym, working out and physically I felt strengthened, afterward I went to a nursing home to visit with a friend from my childhood who is there because of illness, not age related, but is mentally and physically held captive.

Lord, in my small, humble way I held her hands and asked You to help and protect her. The entire day from a spiritual perspective came alive as I felt Your presence with me. As good as I felt about this day, there's a sadness for those I came in contact with, sadness for the position some are in, and sadness because they haven't surrendered to You.

I pray for each and every person I encountered this day, I pray that You Lord, reveal to me the course I should take to improve on this ministry. Lead and guide me all the way, equip me with words that will be meaningful to those who need to hear. I'm committed to Your will and Your way.

> Was not Abraham justified by words when he offered Isaac his son on the altar? Do You see that faith was working together with his works, and by works faith was made perfect? And the scripture was fulfilled which says, Abraham believed God, and it was "accounted" to him for righteousness, and he was called the friend of God. You see that a man is justified by works, and not by faith only.
>
> (James 1:21, 24)

Thank You Lord for Your Word of knowledge and understanding, thank You for allowing me to walk in Your marvelous light, thank You for the maturity that's taking place in my spiritual growth, everyday is a day of thanksgiving I just want to thank You Lord.

Thank You for seeing the real me and not condemning me for the times when on the surface I fell short of Your glory.

Your Word says you'll never leave or forsake me, Lord I'm counting on You.

November 30, 1998

Father God,

I come to You with praise and thanksgiving in my heart; I honor and worship You with every breath I take. I am so grateful for every day that's given to me. I'm so grateful for being able to spend thanksgiving with my daughter and her family in Georgia. It was the perfect time to reflect on how great and wonderful You are. As I observed my daughter's family I was overjoyed with gladness because here was a family that I was a part of and You reign supreme in the midst. Both my daughters are walking in Your light and my heart rejoices.

I pray for all those who have yet to acknowledge You and taste the flavor of Your joy. Father please continue to direct my path and help me to make the right decisions for my well being. I want to do the things that will be pleasing to You and line up with Your plan for my life.

Help me to be more faithful to the ministry You've given me, there are times when I fall short on obedience and I need a push from You, I ask that You trouble my spirit when I'm off course and direct me towards truth and fulfillment.

I know that everything depends on You, and You are first in my thoughts and in my heart, yet I still don't do everything right.

The enemy doesn't want me to succeed but he will not have his way, because I will honor and praise You day and night even when I need guidance and correction, because I know You will not fail me, You will hear me and provide me with all I need for victory.

This little light of mine I'm going to let it shine, the world didn't give it and the world can't take it away.

Teach me to do Your will, for You are my God; Your Spirit is good. Lead me in the land of uprightness.
(Psalm 143:10)

January 2, 1999

Father God,

I want to thank You for being all that You are and for loving me just as I am, so many times I have disappointed You as well as myself. You have clearly given me everything I need to carry out Your will for my life. I want so much to be pleasing to You, yet I continue to wander off track.

Please forgive me and help me be the person You would have me to be, Your plan is the one that always works best. Father help me to stay focused this new year on You and obedient to the things You want me to do for my betterment and for Kingdom building.

I can't do anything without Your help, You know the heart of all Your disciples, please examine mine and know that I want to walk close with You and be an example of how powerful You are.

This year, Lord, I'm going to make every effort to be more of a blessing to You and fill my space with Your love. I have so much to be grateful for and every time I look around I'm aware of all my many blessings. There are so many hurting people in the world, so many that need You and just don't want to make that commitment.

Guide me in the direction necessary to encourage the disenchanted and lonely.

There are times Lord when I am so uncertain about so many things and I just need You to make it clear.

There are times when I feel like I'm just wasting time and accomplishing very little, there are times when my spirit is down and I need Your strength to lean on, there are times when the things that come out of my mouth don't reflect that of a Christian and I'm truly ashamed: so You see father I'm standing in need of a makeover.

This new year do something for me that will help me to be better.

This new year let it show in all I do, all I say, and allow me to shine and sparkle the way You want me to.

This new year start me afresh.

Your Servant

January 11, 1999

Father God,

I just want to rejoice, rejoice in the knowledge of Your truth. You are so special and I just want to thank You for being in my life. There are times father when I am so confused and I need You to clarify things for me. I see so much dishonesty and as imperfect as I am, I often wonder are there any good and real people left in the world.

I wonder how You are going to judge us Father, for as hard as we try most times we still come up short of Your glory. I am not what I should or want to be, and I know to be all that You want me to be I need Your help all the way. I ask You to work on me Lord, work on me, and help me to be the person You want me to be. I know that Your plan for my life is the only plan that will give me fulfillment and joy.

Until I walk in the path that will lead to the fulfillment of that plan I will not have success the way You see success. So here I am Lord leaning on You to continue guiding me and helping me as I stumble along trying to avoid the darts of the enemy as I go.

Let me not forget who I am as your child, Father, let me not forget that You've given me everything I need to succeed, let me not forget that no weapon formed against me shall prosper and that all power is in Your hand and if You be for me then who can be against me.

Let me not forget that when the world says I can't, that You and I comprise the majority.

Let me not forget the power of Your might and that with You all things are possible and that if I continue to keep my hand in Yours as I stumble You will always be there to pick me up.

Father I am so grateful for Your love and faithfulness and I will never turn my back on You because all my hope comes from You.

Thank You for entering my heart.

JANUARY 13, 1999

Father God,

I've allowed myself to stray from the atmosphere that kept me so close to You. I don't like the way I feel, I want to go back to the time when You first took charge of my heart; to the time when all I wanted to do was meditate in the comfort of Your presence. Please guide my steps, take control of my mind, fill my heart with an overflow of Your love. Let wisdom, knowledge and understanding engulf me, use me for Your purpose Lord, use me.

Give me the energy and enthusiasm I need day by day; I haven't forgotten Your goodness and how wonderful You've been to me, You've done Your part, I've faltered on mine.

Forgive me Father, forgive me for disappointing You, forgive me for not acting on the authority You've given all that belong to You, forgive me for doubting You, because when I doubt myself I'm doubting You and what you're capable of. You said in Your word that when I am weak, that's when Your strength sustains us. I believe in You, I'm a witness of Your ability, and yet when I want to do Your will, I still manage to go another way.

Any road that leads away from You is destructive and the only way to peace and joy is in partnership with You.

You've given so much yet I still need more, more help from You.

Help me Lord, help me.

> But You, O Lord, are a shield for me, my glory and the One who lifts up my head. I cried to the Lord with my voice, and He heard me from His holy hill. I lay down and slept; I awoke, for the lord sustained me.
>
> (Psalm 3:3–5)

JANUARY 14, 1999
2:30 P.M.

Here I am Lord,

Back at the place where it all began, when this feeling came upon me to write and express to You what I felt in my heart. I had to begin again Father because I've strayed from being faithful to this calling. I've grown to a higher level from when I first began, but I've slowed down Your process.

I want to ask for forgiveness from You and begin again. Please allow my ministry to advance, point me in the right direction and help me to stay focused.

No one is more important to me then You, no one comes before You Lord, my relationship with You is one that makes everything else in my life work. Help me organize my life so that I can comfortably carry out the things You have in mind for me to do. Direct me to the right bible studies/seminars that will enhance my knowledge, increase wisdom and understanding in my being.

I am so thankful for the level You've already brought me to, I'm so happy in my spirit for the love You've shown me and I hope I can reflect that happiness in my spirit to all I come in contact with.

I want to be an encouragement in representing You

and Your kingdom Father. I'm so glad that You're the most important part of my life and that You always give us another chance, where would I be if you didn't?

Thank You for being all that You are and for opening the door of life for me to enter.

Am I ever so blessed?

> My soul, waits silently for God alone, for my expectation is from Him.
>
> (Psalm 62:5)

March 1, 1999

Father God,

I am so thankful that I have You in my life, there are so many situations to deal with on a daily basis, and I just don't know how I would handle it all alone. I want to be the person You intended me to be, I'm aware of the path You want me to follow, but so often I go the other way.

Help me Father to stay on course, to be a blessing to You in all I do, I want to stay focused on Your program, hide me Lord behind the cross.

Show me, Lord, everyday Your purpose, help me to keep love in my spirit and a willingness to help the less fortunate, to share my blessings with others and the strength and courage to always do what's right. Your Word is true and I see Your promises being manifested in my life, I'm so wonderfully blessed and I don't know how to thank You enough.

I see so clearly Your presence, I hear Your voice and feel Your love, please don't give up on me Lord, please don't give up on me.

> I press toward the goal for the prize of the upward call of God in Christ Jesus.
>
> (Philippians 3:14)

MARCH 6, 1999

> And you shall consecrate the fiftieth year, and proclaim liberty throughout all the land to all its inhabitants. It shall be a Jubilee for you; and each of you shall return to his possessions, and each of you shall return to his family.
>
> (Leviticus 25:10)

Father God,

Today I am so happy, I am so thankful for all that You've given me on this day, Your Word says, "Delight yourself also in the Lord, and He shall give you the desires of your heart" (Psalm 37:4). Father I've carried that scripture with me as I attempted to do Your will, however Father I didn't use that as a reason to be the person You want me to be, because my greatest reward was the feeling I have after helping or encouraging someone in need. I've lost a lot through the years, but I realized that possessions aren't the most important issues in this life. I asked as my number one interest was for divine wisdom, knowledge, and understanding of Your word. Father in Your graciousness I'm receiving that, more and more each day, and I'm so appreciative, thank You so much.

I also know that our personalities stay as they are

and used for Your purpose, so again I thank You for what seems to be a lively and vibrant presence, who most people seem to enjoy, I suppose in Your plan You want me to shine and sparkle, like that of the most precious jewel, the diamond. So here I am processing the desires of my heart which I stopped thinking about long ago as I walk in Your amazing light, a witness of truth and victory for those who believe and maintain a heart that is true.

Father You are so wonderful, I will never stop praising Your name, help me to be the best witness for You and Your Kingdom that I can be, because more than anything else I want to be pleasing in Your sight.

Your servant,

Eunice

March 12, 1999

Father God,

It's me, it's me, it's me Oh Lord, needing You to help me through this life here on earth. I want to be the person You intended me to be but nothing is working out. I've been in a relationship ten long years and in the beginning we were both the same in many ways, but Father You entered my heart and it seems overnight I became a brand new person, You gave me a new attitude towards life, showed me love, the ability to feel worthy and able to accomplish that which is necessary in building Your Kingdom here on earth. Yes old things passed away and new ones emerged.

I've been so blessed in so many ways, but here I am after having been out with those I work with, enjoying dinner and wine at a fine restaurant and good business conversation, feeling low in spirit because my life has a few flaws.

The man I've been with isn't moving in the same direction as I am, and still has the need to be out there searching. What shall I do Lord, what shall I do?

I don't want to be alone, I don't want to be a part of all the mess I see happening between people today, no one seems to be living an honest life, not even Christians, lies, lies, lies, why can't people be contented with each other, why is the search ever present? I realize that the only one I can trust Lord is You, but men and women are supposed to be together, why can't it work or shall I say why does it not work for so many?

I'm a good person, I want to be pleasing in Your sight, yet that man/woman thing is such a let down. Show me lord what I need to know, help me understand and accept the realities of life. Guide me in the right direction for contentment, my mind is open and my heart receptive, I don't want to live feeling like nothing substantial can come from the male gender and that I have to accept this fact in order to get by.

Please don't think I don't trust You Lord, because I do, that's why I'm bringing this to You, Oh Lord I know You're the only one with the answers, I know that in Your plan, only the best will do, and that there's a lesson to be learned from all my experiences, so I ask again, help me to get over this feeling of rejection and disappointment while I wait on You.

Reveal to me the truths that will set me free, put that fire under my feet that will send me on my way, excite my mind to motivation, Oh Lord it's me, It's me, please don't pass me by.

Nothing is impossible for You Lord, I'm Your servant, I want a good life and most of all I want to please You. You said delight yourself in the Lord and You will grant the desires of my heart, I just want to have life more abundantly as You promised, enjoying this Christian walk and fulfilling my responsibilities to You here on earth.

Help me please.

MARCH 12, 1999

1:12 A.M.

Father God,

Here I am wanting to be in your presence; I just came in from meeting with a very good girlfriend, Lord I needed someone to talk to, my relationship with James needs to be discussed, we talked and talked and many issues were brought out, but one thing that was mentioned takes priority over all else, and that was that I should come to You and let You decide and be willing to move on Your direction; Father God have Your way in my life, have Your way, not mine.

Tonight Father we decided to form a support group between women, we discussed many ideas, as to what we would take issue on and try to be helpful with the many things that confront women in today's world, but one thing is sure and that is nothing can work if You're not in it.

So I ask that You come into our plans and make it work for Your glory.

I don't know how Father but I'm depending on You to help me, if I stray on the wrong track, put my feet back on solid ground, direct my thoughts, and guide my path; Oh Lord help me make this work.

I want to be pleasing to You, help me please, You who knows the heart, read mine.

I am Your child, I depend on You, I am imperfect, I can't succeed without You, and I will never try anything on my own, I need Your direction.

Order my steps, Lord, order my steps.

> He heals the brokenhearted and binds up their wounds.
>
> (Psalm 147:3)

May 10, 1999

Father God,

It's me, Lord, it's me; here I am in my late fifties and I realize that the real me is in the inner self that tells me who I am. The sensitive heart You've given me and the ability to love in a way that's beyond my own understanding confirms Your presence; Oh yes there are times when the flesh tries to overtake me, but it only happens for a little while because Lord I'm who I am and my heart responds to that calling.

Sometimes I like myself and sometimes I don't; there are times when I feel like such a disappointment to You, I know You've given me everything I need and more to walk in the plan You've custom made, especially for me, I see it so well yet why do I hesitate?

I see things in myself that astounds me, wonderful things that You've blessed me with and I'm really so grateful; by the world's standards they aren't the things that get you to the top, mostly unnoticed actually, but it's me, it's me and when I stretch out in the beauty of Your gifts I feel so good and the world can't do me harm.

I want to do more for others, I want to be more obedient, I want to put aside foolish thoughts, I want to extend more love and kindness, I want to be all You want me to be, I want to glow in Your brilliance, I want others to recognize that glow for what it represents, I'm Yours Lord and I want the world to know, I live for You, in my heart You know I'm sincere although on the surface it's not always 100 percent visible.

I try Lord, I try but I want to be better, help me Father, help me.

Take away those things that are not for my best interest, You know what they are better than I. Help me to see that which is hindering me, give me strength to walk away from it and give me peace of mind as I move on. If everything I'm surrounded with is a part of Your plan for my growth, then let me realize it and use my authority as a child of God to deal with it, because I know that no weapon formed against me shall prosper.

Help me to stand boldly and speak openly for Your kingdom.

I am who I am Lord, I am the person You've custom made to carry out a mission in my own unique way, I want to do it, I want others to see it and Father most of all I want You to be pleased with me.

With all my love,

Your servant

Me

June 24, 1999

This is the day that the Lord has made I will rejoice and be glad in it.

Father God,

It is time for me to leave for work right now, but I want to take this time to just thank You for being you, thank You for loving me and for all You've done to improve my life. I know You're not finish yet as I have much that still needs improvement, but I'm just so grateful for all that You've done thus far. I'm so much better then I was and it's all because of Your love for me and the fact that You want me to go further.

I love You Lord and I trust You for all the decisions You make for my life; help me to be obedient to Your instructions and help me love more the way You love all Your children.

As I go about this day show me the way to receive all I need this day to make it the kind of day that will honor and glorify You and Your Kingdom.

Bless those who are discouraged and need to hear from You, embrace the sick and all the children in the world that are in need of Your care.

Thank You for the job that I'm going to this morning and bless all those employed there.

In the name of the Father, Son, and Holy Spirit I pray.

Amen

> Your word is a lamp to my feet and a light to my path.
>
> (Psalm 110:105)

June 29, 1999

It's me, it's me, Oh Lord, it's me.

Father God,

I need to speak to You and I need Your help so badly, You know everything about me and my life, those things that please You as well as the things I've fallen short of for Your glory, there are things in my life that I'm not happy with and more than once I've confessed them to You Lord, You have never failed me with an answer only many times I think I don't act on Your advice because I'm afraid to take a chance; Father God I don't know why I feel that way since I know in my heart that You never make a mistake and that Your purpose for our lives is always the perfect solution. Father that's why I'm here again seeking Your strength because I am obviously weak and can't seem to make the right moves.

Help me oh Lord to do just that, make the right moves and trust Your judgment. Today at lunch time as I sat in a restaurant having lunch I spoke with You and asked at that moment to guide me in Your Word with an answer for my present life; my relationship with James, I just don't know how to handle his indifference and the fact that we're just not going anywhere as far as compatibility is concerned, Lord You know the story, and I'm just perplexed about the whole thing since at times I feel I'm in disobedience and other times I feel as if I'm overreacting and that time will bring about a change for the better; am I wrong Lord or am I in denial?

I'm not happy with that situation and I'm also over burdened with debt and can't give to You and Kingdom building the way I should, this adds to my unhappiness and failure to enjoy the peace of being a Christian who loves the Lord with all my heart and soul, and really want to be pleasing in Your sight and move in the direction You desire for me.

Today at lunchtime You gave me Psalm 146 which read:

> Praise the LORD Praise the LORD, O my soul! While I live I will praise the LORD; I will sing praises to my God while I have my being. Do not put your trust in princes, *Nor* in a son of man, in whom *there is* no help. His spirit departs, he returns to his earth; In that very day his plans perish. Happy *is he* who *has* the God of Jacob for his help, Whose hope *is* in the LORD his God, Who made heaven and earth, The sea, and all that *is* in them; Who keeps truth forever, Who executes justice for the oppressed, Who gives food to the hungry. The LORD gives freedom to the prisoners. The LORD opens t*he eyes of* the blind; The LORD raises those who are bowed down; The LORD loves the righteous. The LORD watches over the strangers; He relieves the fatherless and widow; But the way of the wicked He turns upside down. The

> Lord shall reign forever Your God, O Zion, to all generations. Praise the Lord!

Father how can I not understand Your answer and as I do, still need Your help to act on it? But that's the situation and I beg You to intervene mightily, I need Your strength because I'm at a time of weakness. I know there are things I should be doing if I'm going to fulfill Your purpose for my life and maybe James is a hindrance, Your answer tells me that we are not good for each other, but I seem to fear loneliness, help me Lord, please help me.

I've never felt this way about companionship before, why is this happening to me now? I know I can live in victory in whatever way You decide for me, so why can't I activate the separation, and move to the next level of my Christian growth?

You see lord here I am, not functioning at my best only You can make things work, give me the strength. I am Your child, I'm entitled to all the benefits that come with belonging to You and Your Word says when I am weak that's when You are strong for me, and that Your love never stops regardless of how undeserving I am, Lord I want to be happy, I want to be debt free, I want the wisdom and understanding it takes to succeed, Help Me Please!!!

You said: "I will instruct you and teach you in the way you should go I will guide you with My eye" (Psalm 32:8). Lord You said this to me tonight through Pat Robinson and I believe you. I worship, praise and adore You and sincerely thank You for all the blessings You've given me through the years and even as I speak with You now, I thank You for helping me with my confusion; confusion that I caused and need to straighten out. I'm so grateful that I have You to talk with, because all my hope comes from You, man has never stop disappointing me, you're the only one I can trust. In you hands lies my life.

> You will keep him in perfect peace, whose mind is stayed on You, because He trusts in you.
>
> (Isaiah 26:3)

JUNE 30, 1999
12 A.M.

Father God,

I'm going to constantly come to You with this situation between James and I because as You know I need Your strength through all of this, I need You to put people in my presence that will encourage me and help me through this lonely and difficult time.

Most of all Lord I need You to continually speak to me and assure me of Your presence. Tonight I terminated my relationship with James, and Father although we've been together 10 years, I felt an immediate relief and a weight lifted from me, at this moment I feel this is what should happen, we're no good for each other.

I know there will be many moments of real loneliness, but Lord that's where I'm depending on You to come in and handle it, I know You can. I've experienced the peace and joy that comes whenever our spirits meet, I know how powerful You are and that nothing is impossible for You, I ask that You come into my heart everyday and remind me of the strength, power, peace, and joy that surpasses all understanding during the worst of times. I exalt You, Lord, and sing praises to Your name, the name above all names, You are my God, You created me and molded me into this person You see. And You haven't finished yet, I can expect great things from You. Oh Father I thank You, I thank You that I realize that I can depend on You. My life has been so sad where man is concerned, the men in my life came and went and I was left with nothing to build on for the future, but thanks be to You I can have the best future one can ever desire, the fear of death is removed and I have been given the gift of eternal life; I can have success here on earth as defined by Your standards; I can walk in Your marvelous light and have a song in my heart, Oh praise the name of Jesus, praise the Lord!

Thank You for speaking to me tonight through Proverbs 4:20, 22:

> And my son, give attention to my words; incline your ear to my sayings. Do not let them depart from your eyes; keep them in the midst of your heart; For they are life to those who find them, and health to all their flesh.

I'm so happy You are my friend.

July 20, 1999

I will depend on God alone, I will put my hope in Him, He alone protects and saves me. He is my defender, and I will never be defeated. My salvation and honor depend on God; He is my strong protector; He is my shelter. I will trust in God at all times. I will tell Him my troubles for He is my refuge

Amen.

Father God,

Today has been a very bad day for me, My eleven year companion has finalized our break-up. He says he cannot be the man I want him to be. In him I wanted to be loved and cared for, I wanted to retire with him and finally have a chance at a good life with a man, I wanted most of all for him to have a relationship with You, acknowledging You in all things, I thought I could help lead him to You and make our life right. In this last year he made a drastic change in how he handled our relationship, I saw it and didn't like it and when I tried to talk about it with him he just wasn't interested; things were based on a lot of pretense on both sides, so I guess it all had to eventually come to an end and today it did.

Father I am so unhappy, I feel so inadequate as a

woman, the enemy is telling me that my time is up, I'm not attractive anymore and that I won't find anyone at this stage of my life. I know the devil is a liar and that no weapon formed against me shall prosper, but my spirit at this time is at an all time low, please help me, help me to remember who I am in Christ, and that sorrow may endure for a night but in the morning there is joy, help me to get to the joy, this feeling is so painful. I know You have a plan for my life, help me walk in obedience so that I can claim all that You have for me, I can't do it without You.

All my hope comes from You, You are my hope, man has let me down so much in life, but Father don't let bitterness overtake me. I want to always glow and sparkle in Your brilliance; I want the world to know of Your greatness through me. You are the light of the world and I want that light ever present in my spirit.

I know You are going to help me through this, but right now Father I'm hurting so bad, my heart is in such pain and I can't stop the tears, I feel so rejected and I don't know how to handle it, next week I'm attending the T.D. Jakes Conference in Atlanta, Georgia and Lord I'm praying for a miracle from You. I need to be revived; I need to be set free from the evil sprits that are holding me in bondage. I need a refreshing of the soul and I need an uplifting of my spirit to press on towards the mark.

This is jubilee time and I expect to regain all that I've lost, because Your word says so. I stand on Your promises and I thank You so much for being the God that You are, I trust Your decisions and give You all the honor and glory.

Thank You Lord for Your love and mercy.

July 25, 1999

Heavenly Father,

All honor and glory to Your name, I praise You Lord, I lift You up, You reign supreme over all the earth, King of Kings I worship You.

Today Lord, this Sunday, You directed a message to me through Your servant, Rev. Darcel Holloway, she brought me into Your presence as she began her message sweetly singing unto You, Lord, a song. Her point was to sing Your praises in spite of one's despair. When we feel You have forsaken us, sing a song of praise anyhow, because, as her sermon proclaimed, "You are love," and Lord many of us feel that we are not loved and therefore cannot advance in Your kingdom. There are just so many situations and disappointments that our hearts find it difficult to comprehend the enormity of the love You surely have for Your children.

We need to be encouraged and we need Your loving arms around us as we open up our minds to receive. There are so many who have not moved to the place they should be because of feelings of unworthiness; thereby generating the inability to love themselves or comprehend the love You have for us. These strongholds are extremely debilitating and Lord I thank You for the message delivered by Your messenger which stirred up my spirit regarding procrastination. You have given me all that I need and have answered my prayers over and over again, yet I have laid in uncertainty and have not followed through in the areas that You have directed for my advancement.

The disappointments I've encountered from man has affected my progress, but Lord, I know what I know and from this day on I will walk in Your confidence because it's Your strength that has brought me this far and as imperfect as I am, I'm still a long way from what I was.

Your steadfast love has provided a place for me to be the best that I can be and no devil on earth will ever make me feel incompetent. I won't lose sight of my vision, because it's the plan for my success here on earth, You gave it to me, along with a team of Your disciples showing kindness and support, I won't identify with failure.

Lord I have felt lonely so often and unloved that I sometimes forget that during those times it was You who was there for me to talk with; it was You who gave me things to do that would fill the hours with meaningful pursuits; it was You who made me feel special as a person set apart from the worlds standards; it was You who gave me hope even when my mind tried to tell me no one cares; it was You who kept the mustard seed faith growing in my heart so that I couldn't ever completely give up; it was You who allowed me to remain humbled when I was hurt by unkind remarks made by others who showed no sensitivity to my person; it was You who continued to nurture and love me when I was too blind to see; it was You who told me not to worry when rejection from man pieced my heart and made me cry again; it was You who made me see the bigger picture and the cleansing that had to take place; it was You Lord that promised that the desires of my heart will be granted and that I will walk in Your marvelous light.

I will not be able to ever forget what You have done for me, no matter how hard the devil tries to tear me down, he will never succeed, because my Father in heaven is greaten than anything the enemy can bring against me. Any despair I feel will only last for a moment, because I am a child of God and His Word abides in me, I am not doomed for failure, no man can hinder me, I am loved and I can do all things through Christ who strengthens me, and Father forgive me for entertaining the thought that You had forsaken me, I thank You for bringing to my remembrance all the many times You have been right by my side, I've often let You down but You have always been faithful.

You have again set me on the right course for my life spiritually, physically, and mentally, I have the wisdom of balance and as long as I walk in obedience, I can't fail and if I stray for a minute, Your presence is right there to pick me up and set me back on solid ground.

Praise Your name Lord!

Yes, Jesus loves me, yes, Jesus loves me, yes, Jesus loves me, the Bible tells me so.

Enlarge the place of your tent and let them stretch out the curtains of your dwellings; Do not spare; lengthen your cords, and strengthen your stakes.

(Isaiah 54:2, 3)

AUGUST 4, 1999
5 A.M.

Father God,

All honor and praise to You who holds my future in Your hands; I worship You Lord and I thank You for Your presence in my life. I thank You for sending me to the T.D. Jakes Women's Conference; it was the blessing I needed so badly. I felt so encouraged as I absorbed the message You gave each messenger to deliver. I know there are things You want me to do if I am going to walk in Your divine plan, there are situations that have to be dealt with and healing to take place. I will be what You want me to be, I will work on all the areas that need attention, I know You will be with me every step of the way.

The enemy is already telling me I can't, the enemy is trying to steal my joy and insisting that nobody loves me and I'm in this world all alone, but Father today I fasted and took to wailing, because at the conference the emphasis was that wailing women win, I believe that and Lord all day I travailed.

The devil is a liar!

Lord You came to my rescue so quickly, by the end of 24 hours I received a phone call and that call lead to the beginning of communication between the person I have had on my heart and causing me to grieve, immediately a weight was lifted and I felt so much better. I can now concentrate on all the above, thank You, Lord, for loving me so much.

I am going to stay in prayer because I want direction and wisdom to carry out Your will.

More than anything I want to please You and bring honor to Your Kingdom.

I want to be a good person in Your sight and I want to stay on the right path for that to happen. Thank You for the vision I now have, I will do all that is necessary to make it a reality.

If you think I have something to say that people need to hear or read and that a book will deliver Your message through me then I will trust Your decision, I will trust Your direction also for the message to go on the internet, I'm Yours, Lord, use me anyway you like.

It's You and me Lord all the way.

August 6, 1999

> And you have been given fullness in Christ, who is the head over every power and authority.
>
> (Colossians 2:1)

Father God,

All honor, glory, and praise to You, Lord, oh how excellent is Your name, I worship and adore You. As I sit and meditate on You I realize how blessed I am to have a Savior, a Savior in times such as these. A Savior who believes in the least likely and invests in the faltering, I sometimes come under this heading Lord, this esteem demolishing issue hangs over me like a dark cloud and I have to fight to come in out of the expected rain. I know You have done everything in my behalf to show me the victory that is mine in this area. I know as T.D. Jakes mentioned at his Women's conference, I am right now a construction site, until God refurbishes, then I will be complete, until then there's a sign on my back that reads, "Caution-God at work," is there anyone else that feels that same way? Well as low as my confidence can get I know in my heart God that I will see Your confidence in me and it will give me the strength to believe in myself for my destiny.

I know this is true because I believe in You, and I love You with all my heart and soul so I know that the work You began in me will be completed. I'm pressing towards the mark and I have You by my side, I expect to win.

Even though I walk through the valley of the shadow of death, I will fear no evil, for You are with me, Your rod and Your staff, they comfort me, You prepare a table before me in the presence of my enemies.

Tomorrow, Lord, I expect to present myself differently.

Your faithful servant

AUGUST 9, 1999

Father God,

Today is my birthday and later I plan to have dinner with a friend I've known for over 35 years. I look forward to being with her; I need someone to talk to. Right now I know that I need You first and that You are the one that understands my heart and know all before I even begin to express it. You are the one who can also help fix it and Father that's wheat I need; I need You to fix this broken heart.

I'm still trying to keep a relationship going that seems to be doomed, all the signs are there and I just can't let go. I've been in it for eleven years and I love the man, but it's not the same anymore, actually his interests are elsewhere.

We're going in different directions...

I'm hurting so bad because it just won't happen the way I want it to, I can't think anymore, I've been thinking so much about this that my brain is now malfunctioning.

Even when my brain knows what's right my body aches so much that I can't take the correct action, I need Your intervention, Lord, I need You right now.

Help me to know the truth and act appropriately on it.

I want to feel good again, I want to be excited about my future, I want hope, Lord, and only You can give me that.

Please don't pass me by.

August 18, 1999

Father God,

First I give You all honor and glory, I magnify Your name, I praise You to the highest, Lord, and I thank You for all that You are.

Here I am again Father with my mind all tangled up; I am such a disappointment that I wonder how could You love a wretch like me. You've taken so much time with me teaching and showing me so much and making me so much better than I was before, yet I still need Your assurance and right hand to hold me up and help me through tough times and to make the right decisions according to Your standards.

I know what's right yet I still do wrong.

> So I find this law at work; When I want to do good, evil is right there with me. For in my inner being I delight in God's law; but I see another law at work in the members of my body, waging war against the law of my mind and making me a prisoner of the law of sin at work within my members.
>
> (Romans 7:21)

War has been declared on me and, Lord, I just didn't know, I've been trampled on and there I stood allowing it to happen, my self esteem damaged and my mind weakened leaving me to doubt my actions.

I am not lost, I'm Your child, I only have to come to You when I am weak and draw from Your strength, Your Word tells me everything to do when the enemy is invading my space.

I will keep my mind focused on You, Lord, I will remember who I am in Christ and that You have overcome the devil, I was not given the spirit of fear, but of power, love, and a strong mind, I have the authority to rebuke the devil, I will wear the full armor of God, carry the shield of faith and the sword of the spirit, You've equipped me with all I need, I can't lose, besides You are always right there with me, we are the tag team that always wins.

Thank You, Father, for ministering to me, I need You so much.

AUGUST 21, 1999
12:30 A.M.

Lord God,

You are so gracious, so kind, so good I just adore You.

Every day, Lord, You reveal something new to me and I receive it so easily in my spirit, today on Christian radio I heard Your messenger Dr. Charles Stanly; his message was based on Matthew 5:13, which indicates our influence for good as we penetrate the secular society. Lord, I became so interested in this passage and began to understand better my role here on earth, my purpose with those whom I'm constantly surrounded by and understanding on being the light and salt of the earth.

Sometimes I feel that I'm not as good a witness as I should be because I'm not doing or saying enough, but I am walking in the light and that light means so much, it's my best witness for those to see. I also feel that when others can see what You have done for me and how much at peace I am through so many situations then You, Father, are glorified and that is what matters the most.

I pray to You, Lord that I will grow and demonstrate your power and wisdom in all my comings and goings.

I want more love and patience for those who are in

darkness, as I walk through the valley of the shadow of death I will fear no evil for You are with me.

Your Word is alive! And lives in me, I am so grateful, whatever I need I can find in Your Word, when I'm lonely You appear and talk with me, when trouble invades my space, You take control, when my spirit is low, You minister to me and lift me up, when people disappoint me, You give me comfort and understanding of their actions, when I'm bored, You remind me of my ministry and I'm immediately fulfilled when I act on it, when my confidence is at an all time low, You show me all the gifts You've given me in my personality with the ability to love and enjoy a balanced life; and that success by the world's standard is not the same as measured by Yours. I only have to stay focused on You, Lord, and I can rest assured of life more abundantly, I only have to give my heart to You, Lord, and I will never have to worry because You are my shepherd, I shall not want.

> You are the salt of the earth; but if the salt loses its flavor, how shall it be seasoned? It is then good for nothing but to be thrown out and trampled underfoot by men. You are the light of the world, A city that is set on a hill cannot be hidden. Nor do they light a lamp and put it under a basket, but on a lampstand, and it gives light to all who are in the house. Let your light so shine before men, that they may see your good works and glorify your Father in heaven.
>
> (Matthew 5:13, 16)

AUGUST 24, 1999

> If an army surrounds me, I will not be afraid. If war break out, I will trust the Lord. I ask only one thing from the Lord. This is what I want; let me live in the Lord's house all my life.
>
> (Psalm 27)

Father God,

Today as I walked through the streets heading home from work, I thought about my surroundings and how lonely life can be for a Christian. At this moment, Lord, I am not happy, I'm not happy because there is a void in my life and if it were not for my relationship with You I really don't know what I would do.

I want good companionship and it's not happening, I've been deceived and I can't rid myself of the pain, I'm trying to make something work and every indication shows me how difficult it is. Father I need Your guidance plain and simple, I don't know what's right in this situation. Am I ignoring Your instructions and instead following my own mind? Do You want me to stay in this situation until You decide on the right time for changes to take place, does this person need my presence, or am

I fooling myself and need to move on in order for Your plan for my destiny to be manifested? Oh Father what shall I do? Every effort I make just seems to hurt so bad.

This has been an extremely bad time for me, I can't find the energy to go to church the way I should; I stay in Your presence through television, reading Your Word and meditation, I never take my focus off of You, as a result You've comforted me and have been my constant companion.

I know You haven't forsaken me, I know You will help me get back on track, I'm trusting You to complete the good work You've begun in me.

All around me, Lord, I'm aware of the evil that's going on and how decency is vanishing. Most people don't relate to Your guidelines for successful living here on earth. I really feel like and alien trying desperately to survive.

Every day is a struggle to be in this environment, I know there is a lesson in all of this for me, I just want You to help me with this painful period and put in my path that which will deliver me from my depression. I trust You and want only to do what is pleasing to You, yet I feel I'm failing You and myself.

I don't know what has to happen, I don't' have any of the answers, I just want my heart to sing and feel better.

August 29, 1999

Father God,

This week (Friday) I heard the desperation in the voice of a very close and dear friend. She is desperately in need of a financial blessing. She has been praying and doesn't know what to do next. She has received help from a few people from time to time, but what she needs is to be independent of that help and be able to provide for herself.

My spirit tells me that she is not operating in Your wisdom although she has been given the opportunity, but instead follows her own way and never secures any sort of security for herself. This goes back a year and now many changes have taken place in her life and there is no one she can depend on but You.

Depending on You is what we should do, but I see where You have been there for her and as soon as her funds are absorbed, there she is again at day one.

I can't help but think about the parable of the talents, the least one can do is to deposit what we have in a bank and draw interest; that is save something, waiting around doing nothing produces nothing. Your wisdom shows us how to prepare ourselves, and gives us options to consider.

There is always something for us that will help our condition, and we can thank You for that, You provide a way, but we must move on it. We have to know what our priorities are, and that we don't use our resources for vacations, or shopping when we are unemployed and depend on You to rescue us. I know You want us to enjoy life but we also have to show ourselves to be responsible and know that we can't live on the edge all the time.

It hurts me deeply to hear my friend talk about the position she is in and there I am preparing to go on vacation; I knew she needed help, but I couldn't really solve her problem, her problems continue to continue.

I felt that moment that there was a lesson for her to learn and that You would intervene at the time You decided was right.

I know that You love her and so do I. I know that when this is all over she will be a better person and You can fulfill Your plan for her destiny.

If she is obedient to Your voice then Your divine plan for her life I am sure will be manifested.

God please bless her.

And, God, if I am not correct in my assessment please open my mind up for correction by You and my spirit to act according to your guidance.

Thank You for all that you do for me daily in order that I can be all that You want me to be, I pray that one day I will.

Your servant

September 5, 1999

> Then those who feared the Lord spoke to one another, and the Lord listened and heard them; so a book of remembrance was written before Him, for those who fear the Lord and meditate on His name.
>
> (Malachi 3:16)

Most Heavenly Father,

Here I am, Your child calling on You to help me to be a better Christian, to imbed in my spirit the things of You as I meditate on Your Word. I realize that I am in a war and as much as I recognize the evil voice of the enemy attempting to lure me in this direction, I need Your strength. My flesh tells me I am lonely and that I have needs, those causes me to stray away from what I know. Help me to remain strong because the satisfaction I receive in the flesh is fleeting and moments later I am back to feeling unhappy and lonely.

You know the things happening in my life right now, Lord, You know that they don't line up with Your plan for my life, and, Lord, I know that they don't; I am just having such difficulty in letting go and allowing You. I want You more than anything, there is no one I put before You, it's just that I continue to put someone in the plans that doesn't belong there. We are unequally yoked and because I've been with this person so long I can't seem to rid him from my mind. I keep trying to make it work and it's not happening.

I want to function in Your will for my life, so whatever has to happen let it happen, restore peace and joy in my spirit so that I can move on. I will continue to meditate on Your Word day and night hoping that the change will take place; I'm counting on You.

I know how important it is to guard our minds especially since we live in a world of such negativity; and if we're not careful and don't recognize the difference between being entertained and being filled with trash, we will identify with trash and become just that which in turn will reflect in our actions and reactions.

It's so important what we put in our minds, so I'm asking You, Lord, to convict me at every twist and turn of the enemy to invade my mind with trash and ungodly desires. I'm Yours, Lord, and I want to be happy in Your Kingdom. I'm restless right now and I need Your help in maintaining the mind that wins. I will keep Your Word in my head and think on You as I make all decisions.

> And He said, What comes out of a man that defiled a man. For from within, out of the heart of men, proceed evil thoughts, adulteries, fornication, murders, deceit. Lewdness, an evil eye, blasphemy, pride, foolishness. All these evil things come from within and defile a man.
>
> (Mark 7:20, 23)

> The thief comes to steal, kill and destroy
>
> (John 10:10)

God you created me to be a blessing and to have a good life and I will be all that you want me to be and no devil is going to rob me of destiny.

> I have come so that they may have life and have life more abundantly.
>
> (John 10:10)

September 6, 1999

Heavenly Father,

I come to You today with thanksgiving in my heart, I just want to praise Your name and tell You how grateful I am that You are in my life; I give honor and glory to You. When I think about all You've done for me, I can't thank you enough. There have been so many times when I've felt downhearted and if it were not for You I don't know what I would have done. You have always been there for me to tell my troubles to and to lift my spirits up and remind me that there is no problem so big that You can't handle. When I think of how great You are and all that You've created how small my problems become. I'm so ashamed of my complaints and how quickly I seem to forget who my God is.

If I take just a minute to remember then I know that all is well.

Every situation serves a purpose and that purpose always works for my good. I thank You, Lord, I thank You from the bottom of my heart. Please change me so that I can see things the way You want me to, so I can walk in Your will and not mine. I want to be pleasing to You and only You. I want to reflect Your goodness and be an example to others around me. I want to open my mouth and say the things that will glorify You, I want to never forget my authority to cast out demons and rebuke the devil through the precious blood of Jesus The name above every name, the name to which every knee shall bow and every tongue confess that You are Lord, the name that stilled the water, the name that causes the devil to tremble, and the name that gives us the victory in all situations.

I magnify You, Lord, I humbly submit to you. I'm Yours, Lord, use me to Your glory, use me to be a blessing wherever You send me, open my mind to receive all that You have for me, give me the wisdom and understanding to be obedient without hesitation. In this world there is so much grief, raise me above the things of this world. As Your child I have only to ask for what I want, You've given me so much already, but I know I'm not completely there yet, Lord, the enemy continues to invade my mind, help me to be stronger, my heart is sincere, I'm devoted to You, yet I still stumble and fall, pick me up and reinforce my weak areas with Your strength.

You are so wonderful, gracious, and merciful and I am so fortunate to be a part of Your Kingdom, thank You, Lord, oh thank You so much.

> Rejoice in the Lord always, again I will say rejoice! Let your gentleness be known to all men. The Lord is at hand. Be anxious for nothing, but in everything by prayer and supplication with thanksgiving, let your requests be made known to God, and the peace of God, which surpasses all understanding will guard your hearts and minds through Christ Jesus.
>
> (Philippians 4:4, 7)

SEPTEMBER 17, 1999

Father God,

Honor and glory to You, hollowed be thy name, Thy kingdom come, Thy will be done on earth as it is in heaven.

I'm disturbed tonight as I listen to the news reports and hear all that man is attempting to do that is out of line with Your order. These so called Futurists who are predicting the future and all the advanced technology we will have available is scary. I say that because I know You can't be pleased with the way man is going; all these things go beyond how You intend for Your creation to progress. You gave man dominion over the earth to care for and protect it, but the enemy has taken control of man's mind and now man is treading on waters that are dangerous to mankind.

In all man's doings, You have been left out, Your standards for success has been ignored.

As we go into the new millennium I pray that man will come to his senses and seek Your face and counsel. Lord I ask You to extend to me the wisdom to do and say the things that are appropriate for the situations that are before me; Help me to be a blessing and not a hindrance to those who need to move ahead or need encouragement. My heart belongs to You and I humbly submit myself to Your direction.

My life needs improvement and You are the only one that can effect any change that is necessary. Whatever needs to be done I ask You to open my mind to accept and walk in the obedience that will allow Your work to be completed.

Father, I want to extend the ministry You blessed me with to the internet, this vision You gave to me as well in preparing a book, help me to make this vision a reality, one that will bless Your name and do what You intend for it to do for those who come in contact with this ministry.

I see it happening Lord, I've written it down and I've kept it in my thoughts, give me the energy to push on until it happens. Bombard my mind until I follow Your directions, don't allow me to be at peace until it is carried out, show me how I can financially do all things I need to do in order to bless Your Kingdom here on earth. Help me to stay focused and never to forget that I am programmed for success through Your Son, Jesus Christ.

Thank You for Your never failing advice, love, and companionship.

Your servant

> As for God, His way is perfect; the word of the Lord is proven.
>
> (Psalm 18:30)

SEPTEMBER 27, 1999

Heavenly Father,

I worship You with thanksgiving and magnify Your name; there is no other in all the world higher than You, oh how excellent You are, Creator of the Heavens and Earth, as I look around and see Your magnificent creation my heart is overwhelmed with joy and reverence for You, hallelujah, hallelujah, glory hallelujah.

I love You so much, Lord, and I am so unworthy of all the blessings You have bestowed upon me through the years; You have begun a good work in me and I've learned so much about understanding. I know that I have not been obedient to Your every command and my heart grieves on a daily basis because of it. I asked You so many times to help me and direct me, and I must say You've provided me with all the answers over and over again, I just didn't follow Your directions, so again I beg You to forgive me and give me another chance. I will still need Your strength to carry out Your plan and purpose for my life, I'm just so afraid of the pain and loneliness I anticipate feeling. I know I can trust You to know what's best for my life, believe me, Lord, I know Your plan never fails, only those that I do on my own and yet I still walked in disobedience.

I have not been happy and so many situations appear before me confirming the fact that my way is not the way You have in mind. I've been afraid of the future and I know that You hold my future in Your hands, so no harm can come to me, I'm going to step out on faith and watch You go to work on my life. I'm going to enforce what I know about You everyday through the scriptures and rebuke the devil in the name of Jesus to leave me alone. No weapon formed against me shall prosper, I can do all things through Christ who strengthens me, those that wait on the Lord shall renew their strength, I will soar like that of the eagle, I am a child of the King and entitled to all His benefits, a way will be made for those that love the Lord, I will be granted the desires of my heart because I love Him so, He is my shepherd I shall not want.

On my knees I humbly serve and worship You.

October 14, 1999

Heavenly Father,

All glory and honor to You, I exalt You to the highest, how excellent thou are.

Father God I come before You as Your humble servant asking again for direction, asking that You guide me along the path that You want me to take. All too often I make detours and end up making a mess of Your plan. Sometimes I think I'm going the right way only to find out that I was following my own mind and not listening to You. So often You've made it clear, yet I choose to interpret Your message the way I want it to be.

Forgive me, Lord, for my foolishness, it is not my desire to grieve You and I want so badly to be a recipient of Your treasures.

Help me fulfill Your divine plan for my life, help me with obedience, I know it's up to me since You want a willing heart and, Lord, I am willing, yet I still do wrong.

I love You with all my heart and soul, and yet I still do wrong.

I know Your promises and how much You want to act on them and yet I still do wrong.

I feel Your love embracing me every day and yet I still do wrong.

You've given me so much already and yet I still do wrong.

You are my only hope and yet I still do wrong.

You're the only true friend I have and yet I still do wrong.

In my darkest moments You offer peace and comfort yet I still do wrong.

You show me clearly all the proper steps to take yet I still do wrong.

You give me one chance after another, waiting for me to finally do it Your way and loving me all the while, picking me up, dusting me off and starting me all over again.

How did I come to deserve all of this from You?

Thank You, Lord, for loving me anyway.

Eventually, Lord, I'll do right, I promise You I'll never stop trying.

November 6, 1999

Father God,

Here I am, Your confused child who wants more than anything to be pleasing to You, but feeling like Your biggest disappointment.

I love You more than anyone or anything, You are my God, and there is nothing greater than You. You give hope to the hopeless and encourage the disenchanted, You move in our minds and a change takes place in our hearts, You give us peace and joy during the most turbulent times and when we forsake You and go our own way, You open Your arms and welcome us back unto yourself, oh how special You are to those who know You and realize the magnitude of Your greatness.

You've placed so many thoughts in my mind and, Father, I want to act on them; I want to make these visions come into manifestation. I want to bring glory to You and Your Kingdom, I want to be Your fruit-bearing disciple. Direct me and make available resources that will make Your plan work; I want to do more, Lord, please help me.

I see so many things now, Lord, that I feel You are involved with, I hunger for a meaningful Christian life, I want to be all that You want me to be, right now I'm not and I need Your help. I can do nothing without You; show me the way.

If I have to stay on my knees day and night, I will Lord, I will, if I have to fast until I'm weak from hunger, I will Lord, I will; if I have to wail and wail and wail some more, I will Lord, I will. I am your servant and You make promises to me, I know there are requirements of me, but You promise to love and care for those with a heart that is true, and Lord, my heart belongs to you. The enemy attempts to make me fail, but he's a liar, I can't fail because of who I am in You and Your name alone is more than enough for victory.

I stand as I am, depending on you, the one who knows all my troubles and all my desires only You can work out my life to reflect the goodness and love You have for me.

December 2, 1999

> I have become as a wonder to many, but You are my strong refuge. Let my mouth be filled with Your praise and with Your glory all the day.
>
> (Psalm 71:7,8)

Father God,

How excellent is Thy name, I give You all the honor and glory, Father, for there is none other greater than You. I want to thank You, Lord, for Your guidance, I want to thank You for putting me on the path of righteousness, for opening up my mind and heart to receive Your Word in my spirit and to thirst everyday for more.

I thank You, Lord, for the people You've put in my presence that have helped me to grow so strong in the faith, many of them don't know the impact they've made to my spirituality.

Just being in the presence of the saints, observing and hearing the many testimonies and being in agreement to where our hope lies and where our blessings come from is a powerful message to my soul, I thank You, Lord, I thank You.

Lord I draw from all the many experiences and ways in which the people of God praise and trust You through all the many situations they face on a daily basis. The elderly that I have been blessed to share time with have taught me so much. One of the old spirituals sung in the black church express it wonderfully.

In their own words they say: "they've been running for Jesus a long time and don't feel no ways tired, I've come too far from where I started from, nobody told me the road would be easy, I don't believe He brought me this far to leave me, cause everyday with Jesus is sweeter than the day before, and I don't mind the pitfalls cause every time I get to one He's right there, so daughter I don't feel no ways tired, cause I've come too far from where I started from, nobody told me the road would be easy, I don't believe He's brought me this far to leave me."

Thank You, Father, for the faith and spirit I witness in that old time religion that I'm holding on to in my Christian walk.

December 14, 1999

My Lord, my Savior, my Redeemer,

I am just a person, Lord, just a person, and this person is trying so hard to love and all I ever wanted was someone to love me back, but something always happens and I'm left alone and hurting.

After eleven years with someone I am hurting again.

Father, I thank You for removing that person from my company, because You saw that on my own I couldn't do it, and I knew he was a hindrance to my spiritual growth, only I didn't want to face the loneliness and pain involved with departure. I just wanted someone I could be the woman I am and share the love I have to offer.

Am I foolish to believe that two people could just want each other forever and always be excited with each others company?

Why, Lord, has it been so difficult for me to find happiness in my relationships that aren't just a passing fancy? Even the long terms have slowly fizzled out.

What I wanted seems so simple, but I've never been able to acquire it. Lord tell me what is Your plan for my life, I need to know, because sometimes I feel like just giving up and I just don't know how to handle it.

You've done some wonderful things for me, this I

know, but, Father, I'm beginning to feel inadequate and useless and very lonely. I miss my mother so much and without her to love and enjoy, there's no one else. My daughters are so far away and besides they have their own lives to live, where do I fit in?

I see Your hand in everything I do, and although I don't understand it all I know it's for my good. If I didn't have You to talk with and count on for strength I don't know how I would survive. I'm so thankful for the only relationship that I know won't die.

I'm so thankful for Your Word; for always reminding me especially during my darkest moments that I'm not ever really alone. I'm just so disappointed in my affairs of the heart and now here I am starting all over again trying to make myself satisfied.

Father help me to be strong and exercise the faith that I have in my being for You, Your word said faith as small as a mustard seed will do, but mine exceeds that and my love for You is boundless, I know I can't turn around so please help me through these times.

Precious Lord, take my hand, lead me on, let me stand, I am tired, I am weak, I am worn; Through the storm, through the night, lead me on to the light, Take my hand, precious Lord, lead me on.

December 24, 1999

Father God,

During this last month of the year 1999 I want to stand up and talk openly by way of paper and pen because that's the way You first revealed to me that I could say something that would glorify Your Kingdom, encourage others and help me to grow in my relationship with You.

Father, I want to openly thank You for taking control of my life and putting me on the path to be the best that I can be, not by the worlds standards but by Yours. I admit Lord that I don't always understand everything You do, because my understanding is not on the same level as Yours, but I know deep in my heart that everything that happens is in Your divine purpose.

I've had much heartache and there were times when I wondered how could You use me to help me encourage others when my own life is not altogether correct? But with each episode in my life I've come out wiser and have a little bit more I can share with those who need to hear, I thank You so much for not giving up on me; Your word says: "For I know the plans I have for you, says the Lord. They are plans for good and not for evil, to give a future and a hope. In those days when you pray I will listen.

You will find me when you seek me, if you look for me in earnest" (Jeremiah 29:11, 13).

I know of Your faithfulness to those who love You and I come, Lord, I come. In this world with so much evil abounding, we the people of God can't sit in our comfort zones, we must be committed to sharing the Gospel to those that are lost, help me help all who claim Your kinship to be effective witnesses. Open our hearts to kindness, understanding, and love.

We depend on You, Lord, You are our hope, You are our protector, our defender, our shelter, our refuge, our salvation and honor depend on You, we the people of God will trust You in all things and come to You with all our concerns, because only You can make a way out of no way, only You can fix the mess we get ourselves into, only You can give us peace during the worst of times, only You, Lord, the one who knew us while we were still in our mothers womb and who knows every hair on our heads, only You who created the Heavens and the Earth, and everything therein, only You, the Great I am, Wonderful Counselor, King of Kings, Lord of Lord, Alpha and Omega, whose name is Jesus, the sweetest name we know, and has all power in Your hands.

We praise You, Lord, we exalt You, we worship, honor, and adore you, we open our hearts to You for cleansing, to be renewed and revitalized to do Your will and walk in Your ways. Bless us, Lord, and help us as we function in our efforts to do good in a wicked world, and that our light will shine so that we will be recognized as Your disciples.

I pray for unity among all people and that we will one day worship You together in love.

December 29, 1999

Father God,

As this year comes to an end I just want to come into Your presence with gratitude and thanksgiving. I want to exalt Your name and give You all the honor, for there is none greater than you. I think about all the many times when life was just beating me down and so often there was no one whom I could express the real me to. You were always there to comfort me and show me a way to correct or change the situation. During my lowest moments You lift me up and remind me that as a child of Yours I will have a rewarding life because You are in charge.

I'm so happy about that since on my own, I know I can accomplish nothing. I thank You for the renewing of my mind and the overflow of appreciation and love for the simple things in life that are so often taken for granted. There was a time when my concept of success was measured by all the wrong things and I spent years feeling inadequate, but You ministered to me, and in Your sweet, kind way showed me that when we walk on the path that You paved for us, we no longer feel like less then we are, or intimidated by others accomplishments or possessions.

We are all a part of the body of Christ and we all

serve equally in building Your Kingdom here on earth. I'm eternally grateful that as I gain more and more understanding and knowledge I don't have to worry about the world's system or views, and even if the road is long and narrow, I'm satisfied because You and I are the team that wins.

You love and care for me when no one else will, You attend to my needs and shower me with an abundance of favor and give my life meaning. As I reflect on this year, I realize that it has been a blessing in so many ways; because even when I didn't think so, I had another dimension added to my profile when I went through tough times that helped me to be a better person in understanding and wisdom that could possibly help someone else along the way.

I don't have all the answers, Lord, and the mysteries belong to you; I just thank You again for Your spirit in my soul and Your love that's growing in my heart.

For the new year I commit to being a better Christian and obeying Your voice, Lord, I just need Your help and strength in my efforts and because of who You are, I know I can depend on You; because You want us to soar on eagles wings, sparkle with the brilliance of a diamond, and fulfill our destiny.

No, I don't feel no ways tired, I've come too far from where I started from, nobody told me, that the road would be easy, but I don't believe you brought me this far to leave me.

March 6, 2000

Oh my Lord, my Father, my majestic One,

Here I am, Father, at Your feet, asking for the comfort of your embrace, I need You so much. My life seems to be failing apart, I can't make myself contented, because I have been deceived by the man I love, I can't continue feeling like this and do the work You have destined me to do. My heart is broken and I don't know how to repair it, I am tormented every day and night, yet on the surface among others and even the man that is hurting me so much, I pretend that everything is fine, but inside the hurt is eating away at me like a cancer, the enemy has activated his attack full force and bombarding my spirit with the fear of growing old and unappealing to anyone, nothing can seem to make me overcome this feeling of uselessness no matter how hard I try. Only You can restore me back to the person You intended me to be. You gave me a lively and vibrant personality to use according to Your purpose in leading souls to You and Your Kingdom, and Father, I thank You for that because You made me realize that all those years I spent feeling insignificant and incompetent that my life did have a purpose and that purpose was going to be fulfilled and bring glory to You. Although I didn't always do the right things You continued to bless me, help me and allowed me to start all over again, You've been a kind and loving Father to an undeserving, and many times disobedient servant.

If You look inside my heart You know that I want to be all that You want me to be, that I sincerely love and worship You in spirit and truth, I attend to Your Word and thirst after knowledge and understanding; I want to be a good woman for You, Lord. You are the God that makes everything possible and the only one that can mend this aching heart, I give this problem to You and I will depend on You alone, I don't believe You brought me this far to leave me.

I feel like I'm living in a world that makes it so difficult to lead a good and godly life, but I know that when we give our lives to You then the impossible becomes possible; I've seen it so often and I believe in my heart that even I can be the woman You want me to be, regardless of how fierce the attacks of the enemy becomes, You reign supreme over all the earth and have equipped us to boldly stand up to the devil and declare victory in the name of Jesus, and even in our weakness Your strength is made known.

I believe that You will supply all that I need to overcome this broken spirit and also bring those in my presence that will help me along the way and somewhere along the line, this experience will turn into a blessing that I can use to help others who are dealing with the pain of a broken relationship and need the compassion of someone who knows.

I know who You are, I know what You can do, I know that with all You give to us we are still fighting the flesh and we can conquer it with Your help. It's a fight that is ongoing day by day, but praise be to You, we can win.

> We are hard pressed on every side, but not crushed; perplexed, but not abandoned; struck down, but not destroyed.
>
> (2 Corinthians 4:9)

I am who I am because I belong to the One who created me, the King of Kings, I can do all things because You strengthen me and with You all things are possible, You did not give me a spirit of fear but of power, love, and a strong mind, no weapon formed against me shall prosper, I wear the whole armor, therefore I can withstand all the evil that comes my way, I will never forget all that You've done for me, and all You're still doing for my betterment, therefore I'm committed to You and trust You completely, You want me to reflect all the riches that comes from You because all that's good and perfect I'm entitled to as an heir in Your Kingdom, I will wait on You, for You know what's best for my life I will depend on Your decisions and never my own.

What a friend we have in Jesus, all our sins and griefs to bear! What a privilege to carry everything to God in prayer.

March 7, 2000

Father God,

Here I am just one day after feeling so down and out shouting hallelujah! Praise be to the God of Heaven and Earth! Praise You for loving me and comforting me in my hour of loneliness and despair; for reminding my spirit that my life stands for something and will be about my Father's business which surely spells victory and success!

I am somebody; I am worth loving and have much to offer only because of the blessings my Father abundantly gives me on a daily basis. Everyday is another opportunity to move forward towards my destiny. I will have all that is promised to me; my heart rejoices because my cup runneth over.

Today I felt like my spirit was renewed and I see myself exploring the areas that You, Lord, intend for me to activate. I can do what You, Lord, want me to do because You've provided all that I need to succeed.

If I keep my mind focused on You, Lord, I can take the necessary steps without any fear.

If I am patient I can make the right decisions as directed by You, if I am diligent and prayerful in my efforts I will not grow weary; my mind is open for all kinds of new insights, I believe in miracles and the power of the supernatural. Lord, You intend for me to use the tools You provided for me to win; together You and I are the tag team that always come out on top. No weapon formed against me shall prosper, and anyone that harms Your anointed will suffer.

God has called me for his special purpose and that purpose will be fulfilled.

This little light of mind I'm gonna let it shine, let it shine, let it shine, let it shine.

April 4, 2000

Oh my Lord and Savior, Jesus Christ,

Here I am at Your mercy needing comfort that only You can provide, my life has been in such a state of confusion and I don't know what to do to gain control. I thank You every day for being at my side through it all, because without my awareness of Your presence I don't know how I would make it from one day to the next.

I'm so thankful that I have You to talk with when my heart is in so much pain, I'm so grateful to You for that relief. I suppose only time will heal what I feel, and as difficult as it is, I know You will help me with it.

I need Your wisdom to guide me through the paths that have been laid before me, some lead only to destruction and others may be right for me, only I'm not sure.

Penetrate my mind with the right way to go, don't let me continually make foolish choices. I want to live a good and fulfilling life that reflects Your glory and exalts You on high, but I so often just plainly mess up.

Lord, I've had so many unhappy times in my life, please show me and help me do the right thing this time. If You know my heart You know that I really want to be a good servant and that I am never comfortable sinning against You. I cry out to You in agony when I know I've done something that is unpleasing to You. This world is so cruel and hard, people everywhere are just doing what they want with no thought of You, there isn't a lot of support for the righteous, and this life can be oh so lonely.

You didn't intend for us to live alone, when You created man You saw that man was lonely and needed someone, well I need someone, someone who will appreciate me, the person You made me to be; send me that person and most of all help me to recognize that person when he appears.

"I will never leave or forsake you, delight yourself in the Lord and He will grant you the desires of your heart."

It's me, it's me oh Lord.

APRIL 22, 2000

Father God,

Here I am again, I just want to honor and praise Your holy name, I just want to come into Your presence with thanksgiving. I humble myself before You and reach into my heart with sincere appreciation for what You went through for an undeserving person like me.

During this Passion Week I cry out to You with love and I give reverence to my almighty God, I'm so glad You did what You did otherwise where would I be? This week above all weeks I give my total concentration on You, Lord, I open my heart and my ears to all that relates to You; this is such a precious time for Your followers and I am honored to be among them. I think about how faithful You have been to me especially during this last year when I felt so disappointed and betrayed in my relationship with the man in my life, You never left my side, You spoke to me over and over again in Your effort to help me move on to the place where You wanted me so I could finally fulfill Your plan for my destiny and experience the peace and joy in store for me when we do things Your way, only I struggled so much in being obedient, but You never gave up on me, You tried several ways, but my heart just wouldn't listen, You continued to help me, until I took notice. Thank You for putting someone in my path that would have an affect on me when I needed it so much; it was You through someone else moving me on.

This life can be so upsetting and stressful, but You will always sustain those that belong to You and I love You so much for that. I have been through a lot, my self esteem suffered, I began to doubt myself and my ability, but You wouldn't let me sink to rock bottom, You provided what I needed to learn, grow, and press on. You are so good and so worthy of all the praise; I praise You, Lord, I praise You in the morning, I praise You in the noonday and all through the night, I praise You, Lord, and I thank You for what You've done for me.

Guide me, let Your Holy Spirit teach me and direct me to do what will bring honor and glory to You, help me keep this light in me shining for the world to see Your presence in me, help me to response properly as a Christian to those in distress, help me to keep a clean heart, to love those who are difficult, to remember who I am in Christ thereby never giving in to the wiles of the devil. Because this week is the most prevalent for our Christian faith this week tells us that You are the true living God, and all power is in Your hands, this week tells us that we have the victory and that we can do all things through You, this week reminds us what You went through to save us, so that we can have a future and hope. This week tells us of Your great love and we are to set ourselves apart and bear the fruits of the spirit so that all will know that we are Your disciples. This week we should all thirst for more knowledge, more understanding, more love for all people, because we know that it was Your grace and mercy that brought us through. This week we bring to the surface all unforgiveness we've carried for those who know not what they do to hurt others in so many cruel and vicious ways, instead we pray for their deliverance from the clutches of the enemy, and as we do that our spirit will be in line with Yours. This week we surrender all to You and commit ourselves to Your service and obedience to Your word.

April 23, 2000
3:30 a.m.

It's me; It's me Oh Lord,

I can't sleep, I can't stop thinking of Your greatness and how You rescue Your children from harm, Your Word says "don't do any harm to my anointed," I am one of Your anointed and harm was taking place in my life. I was so distraught and feeling so low and unappreciated, my heart was pulled out of my chest and trampled on, my mind was receiving messages of defeat and worthlessness, I didn't love myself and didn't know how to pull myself together.

But my Lord, my Savior, my Bright and Shining Star, You allowed all this to happen in order for me to get to the place You wanted me to go, no, You didn't make this happen, the devil was behind it all, but since I wouldn't listen to Your voice, You let the devil have his way for a little while; just long enough to make me realize how much I needed You and to fall on my face in desperation for Your help. Yes, I now thank You and all that happen to me if that is what it took to bring me to this point. I am somebody, I'm a child of the King, equipped to fight off serpents and all the principalities of spiritual warfare. I have the sword of the spirit and no evil can befall me, greater is he that is in Me than he that is in the world, at the sound of Your name, Jesus, the devil must flee, yes I once was blind but now I see, and far beyond my understanding You continue to love me in spite of myself. I'm so grateful for that love, I'm so grateful for another chance to be happy and for the uplifting of my spirit and all that I've been through I can still have joy.

I cried, I suffered, I wailed in agony and You heard me, You had mercy and You delivered me from all that pain, thank You, Lord, thank You.

I'm so relieved, I can go on with my life, I can be the person You want me to be, I'm back on the path You prepared for me, oh Lord, thank You, use me, Father, for Kingdom building, here I am, use me.

APRIL 30, 2000
3 A.M.

Be merciful to me, O Lord, for I cry to You all day long, rejoice the soul of Your servant, for to You, O Lord, I lift up my soul.

(Psalm 86:3, 4)

It's me, it's me.

Father I come to You again and again, because You are the only one that can help me make sense of my life and the things that come about. I don't know the reason why everything is seemingly turned upside down, so much has happened and changes are taking place, I pray that the changes that are happening are a part of Your divine intervention in maturing me and moving me to the next level for Your purpose.

I hear Your voice in all that I do, I know You are with me and want me to be happy, I thank You so much for moving me past the heartache I've experienced and onto being uplifted spiritually and reminded that I am special to You and that You have a plan for my life and in that plan I will do the work successfully.

I don't know all the answers, my understanding is

limited, but I do know that if it's about Your business then I don't have to know more about, rather trust You and You alone.

I've been hurting for so long that I pray and cry out to You to guide me in the right direction, I can't depend even on myself anymore for knowing if I'm really hearing from You or hearing what I want to hear. I feel that this year will be very meaningful in my life and my relationship with You, I feel that You wanted my full attention and that now You have it, I know my heart is sincere, I know that I want contentment and want to please You above all else, I know that somewhere in this life I will walk in Your success, because You never give up on those whose heart is true.

> You did not choose me, but I chose you and appointed you that you should go and bear fruit, and that your fruit should, that whatever you ask the Father in My name He may give you.
>
> (John 15:16)

Thank You for all You've done for me, I praise You, Lord.

May 9, 2000
10:40 p.m.

Oh Lord,

You are so good to me, all within a twenty four hour period not only did You give me an answer to my despair, but You also made me aware of how I'm already blessed and have so much to be grateful for. As I laid on my bed after a busy and stressful day I began to watch a program about prison life, and in my wildest imagination I can't visualize or attempt to understand the feeling one has in an incarcerated situation, and at that moment I realized how blessed I am. Free to go about my business and free to make decisions and choices. You gave us our free will and yes so often with that free will we set ourselves up to be used by the devil, who roams about looking for those to devour, destroy, and kill, many fall into a bottomless pit.

I thank You for being the God that You are because You still offer hope to all who decide to follow You, even those who are jailed, you can still give them peace and the ability to handle the punishment, because we still have to pay for some of the things we do.

Although You may hate some of our actions, Lord You still love us and will give us comfort when no one else will. You make an impossible situation bearable, and give us joy in our heart, You give us something to meditate on and allow us to bear fruit. We can contribute to Your kingdom and feel like a person again, not an outcast, my Lord, You are so awesome in Your effectiveness, there is none other like you in all the earth and I magnify the name of Jesus.

I've been encouraged and know that I must make the most of this time You've given me. There are so many around me that are despondent, so many who have yet to realize where their hope is, I must reach some of those souls and help lead them to You, help build up their faith, help them see the glory of You, Lord, see all the possibilities, see and appreciate the wonder of Your universe, the many ways we can succeed when we put You first and allow You to come into our heart.

I am so blessed and I know it, Lord, forgive me for the times when I allow the enemy to creep into my space and attempt to destroy my relationship with You, I say attempt because nothing will even separate me from You, during my valley moments You always rescue me when I call on Your name, Jesus, Your love is unconditional and I am so happy to belong to You.

With Your help I will move forward and I will say it as often as I need to because I don't want to forget that I can do all things through Christ who strengthens me.

You are the Rock in a weary land.

May 9, 2000
12:55 a.m.

Oh God,

It's me and I cry out to You to hear me, I'm fasting and praying in order to get Your attention, in order for You to know the sincerity of my heart, in order for You to have mercy on me and help me make something out of my life. Renew my mind with the right thoughts and direct my steps in the right direction. I don't want to live a worthless defeated life, I have a great capacity to love, You know that, Lord, You custom designed me in my mother's womb, help me develop that love so that it will serve a purpose that will be pleasing to You and bring honor to Your Kingdom.

I've wasted so many years stumbling about in all the wrong places, seeking affection from the wrong arms, and feeling so stripped and empty in the end, and my heart was always left damaged. You embraced me and began to make changes, You gave me hope in all areas. Lord, I thank You so much; You allowed me to see the possibilities of a wonderful and successful life when we put our trust in You and are obedient to Your word; only, Lord, so often obedience was a problem for me; I don't always listen and obey, and because of that I still suffer the worlds punishment and come back to You hurt and broken needing restoration. So, Lord, here I am again, with a spirit that has suffered but not destroyed, I know there is good in me, I know You can help me to succeed in being a blessing, I know a lot about Your Word and I know it's truth, I know that growth is taking place in me in spite of myself, I've got some hard lessons to learn, but I yield, Lord, I yield.

I can't fight this feeling any longer, I beg You to take away this pain I'm feeling over what I know was a bad relationship for me and Your purpose for my life, help me, Lord, to just plain get over it!

I want the right spirit in order to move forward, I want to be determined to do Your will, I want to see Your plan and Your hand in all my actions so clearly as not to be denied. I want to feel good again, I want to be the me You want me to be, I agonize over this cloud that hangs over me, I depend on You and all that's presented to me through Your Word and all those who come into my presence as Your messengers, I beg You to lift this weight off of me and grant me the desires of my heart (psalm 37:4). Father I was just lead to read again that passage from Psalm 37:4 only I read a little further on to verse 5, 6, 7, 8, 9, 10, and 11, Lord, is this an answer from You? Your word is true and will not return to You void, so I stand on those verses and I remember all others that reinforce who You are and what You are capable of; I will continue to fast and pray for a while because I want You to know that I can sacrifice, I can bring my petitions to You as in the days of old because You are the same yesterday, today, and forever.

I will enter your gates with thanksgiving in my heart I will enter your gates with praise, I will say this is the day that the Lord has made I will rejoice and be glad in it. Your praises will continually be in my mouth.

May 23, 2000

My Lord, my Savior,

I want to thank You for the wonderful vacation You've given me, I needed it so badly, and because You are so aware of our needs You always come through for Your children. I was blessed in being able to go on a cruise with my oldest daughter along with a couple of her friends, all of whom are saved and it was such a blessing to be in good Christian company, thank You so much.

I had time on this vacation to think about my life and to ponder on where I think I want my life to go at this time, only, Lord, I just know that I want to be happy, I just know that after all the disappointment I've been through that it won't be easy for me to trust relationships, and, Lord, I just want to be on the right track; so here I am again praying for Your guidance as I've been doing through all my many ups and downs. I only trust You but I need to be sure that my actions are directed by You and not by my own foolish mind.

You've given me Your wisdom but because I don't always act on it, I just keep coming back to You for confirmation. Please continue to hold me up and help me to stay where I belong.

I don't know what to do next, I don't know where my happiness lies; I just don't want to feel confused.

Only You can unscramble the complexities I bring into the picture.

The only thing that remains true in my heart is my love for You and that I want to be pleasing in Your sight; I've failed many times in pleasing You, but I'm so glad that You always welcome me back into Your bosom, forgiving me and comforting me, what a great God I serve.

Thank You, Father, thank You.

I am the clay and You are the potter, shape me into Your desired mold and use me for Your glory.

If I am wandering in harm's way, protect me and redirect my steps, do all that it takes to make me the person You want me to be, I'm Yours, Lord, and I give You all the honor, all the praise, all the love and loyalty that's within me and nothing will ever separate me from You.

Your servant,

> Our soul waits for the Lord; He is our help and our shield.
>
> (Psalm 33:20)

June 10, 2000

Oh Most Heavenly Father,

Today like all other days I have You on my mind, I awake thinking about Your greatness and how blessed I am to be a part of Your kingdom. Thank You for allowing me that privilege. Thank You for putting a hedge around me and sealing it with Your protection against all evil, so that no bad thing can overpower me.

> For all the promises of God in Him are yes and in Him amen, to the glory of God through us. Now He who establishes us with you in Christ and has anointed us is God. Who also has sealed us and given us the Spirit in our hearts as a guarantee.
>
> (2 Corinthians 1:20, 22)

I have all I need living in me for success in all areas of my life here on earth.

> Your word is a lamp to my feet and a light to my path.
>
> (Psalm 119:105)

Your Holy Spirit will guide me into all truth, I can depend on You at all times to know good from evil and right from wrong, so I live without excuse, I carry Your word in my heart. I pray that You will continue to help me with complete understanding with that which I need to know to minister to others and to deliver the good news: to Your glory.

I am not a scholar, my wisdom comes from You, I will open up my mind for growth, my heart for acceptance and reverence to You for who you are and the great work You're accomplishing through me, because I know I am nothing without Your presence.

Thank You, Lord, thank You for just being available for me to talk to, the world is just so lonely.

Time is filled with swift transition, naught of earth unmoved can stand, build your hopes on tings eternal, Hold to God's unchanging hand! Hold to His hand, hold to his hand build your hopes on things eternal, hold to God's unchanging hand! Trust in Him who will not leave you, what so ever years may bring, If by earthly friends forsaken, still more closely to Him cling! Hold to his hand, hold to his hand build your hopes on things eternal, hold to God's unchanging hand.

Yes God is real for I can feel him here in my heart.

June 12, 2000

Father God,

First I rejoice in the name of Jesus, oh hallelujah, I just worship and adore You, I sing Your praises all day and all night, my heart is filled with love for You.

This week I will speak with two people that are a part of my personal life, You know who they are and all about the things that transpired between us, so I don't have to explain all of that, I just ask that Your Spirit that dwells in me will be activated by me there by guiding in the way I should go, that my decisions will be correct and not hinder my destiny. I trust You, Lord, but I don't trust myself.

It's not Your fault we know, You've been by my side all along reminding me of all that You've put in me for strength, growth, maturity, and power, however my disobedience have caused me all of my unhappiness in these matters.

Have mercy on me and help me remain strong through Your power, I am nothing without You and I need You every hour. I pray that all my steps are ordered by You, I want to be all that You intend for me to be, I will keep my mind stayed on You, I will delight myself in You, I will meditate on Your word and carry it in my heart, don't give up on me, stay with me until the day of completion of the good work You began in me.

Thank You for all that You've done so far and all that You're still doing on my behalf day by day.

Your servant

JUNE 28, 2000

My Lord, My Father,

I come to You with a sincere heart, I come to You asking for your intervention in my confused life, confusion that I probably caused and the enemy joined in fulltime. I want to know that I'm moving in the direction You want me to go, I need to know that my destiny will come into being and that I will glorify You and help build Your kingdom here on earth. I confess that I don't know the right way to go, I need You to direct me and I need to be in Your presence every day.

I want You to flood my mind with Your word, I want You to protect that which You have put in me and I need to know what I know without any doubt.

I stand firm on my faith in You, on who You are and what You're capable of. In my weakness You are strong, please demonstrate Your strength in me, please help me to be a blessing to You and remove all strongholds that are preventing me from advancing in my ministry.

I pray for deliverance from slothfulness and disobedience, I want to move forward and be all that I can be through You and for You.

Hear me, oh Lord, Please hear me!

Fear not, for I am with you; be not dismayed, for I am your God. I will strengthen you. Yes I will help you, I will uphold you with My righteous right hand.

(Isaiah 41:10)

July 15, 2000

My Father, my Lord, my God,

As I open my eyes to a brand new day, I take a deep breath and give honor, glory, and thanksgiving to You for allowing me to be here and able to face whatever challenges I may face on this day. I don't anticipate any problems, but instead look forward to being a blessing to someone in whatever small way that I can. I am equipped to handle anything the devil might have in mind to spoil my day. It just won't happen because Your Spirit dwells in me and I intend to be recognized by the fruit that I bear.

You've been so good to me and everyday I'm amazed at the growth that has taken place as I study to make myself approved, as I may not be all that I should be, but You have brought me a long way from where I started.

I depend on You, Lord, and I have no fear, because at my lowest point, I can still have joy. You see, I believe Your Word to be true, so I stand on all Your promises, and know that as I delight myself in You, You will grant me the desires of my heat. I see that happening everyday, and if You never did, I will love You anyway, because in my trusting in You, I know You look out for my best interest, and Your understanding is higher than mine, but this I know, that You are with me always, Your Word says:

> For the Lord your God is a merciful God. He will not forsake you nor destroy you, nor forget the covenant of your father which He swore to them.
>
> (Deuteronomy 4:31)

This I carry in my heart, soul, and spirit, so when hard times occur, adverse situations, sickness, death, and disappointment from others, I walk in victory because You and I are the tag team that wins.

July 24, 2000

Father God,

Here I am, just the way I am, and I'm not happy with myself, I'm not happy because I feel like such a disappointment to You and myself. I want to be the person You designed me to be but I just keep getting off track and setting myself back instead of moving forward. I've tried to fast and pray so that You will know the sincerity of my heart and I can't even make it through the day with the fast, why am I having such a hard time? Why can't I discipline myself and show that I have strength in something? Father, if You know my heart, and I know You do, You also know that I am for real.

Help me to be a better person, help me to walk in the strength of Your power, to be seen as Your chosen vessel, bringing glory and love to Your name. I want to be refreshed; I want my mind and spirit elevated to the next level of growth in knowledge, understanding, love, wisdom, and strength.

I sit under Your teaching everyday and I hear, oh Lord, I hear, I absorb and try to apply as well as I can, only I need divine intervention, help me, please help me!!

Don't let me attend this upcoming seminar only to

return the same as I felt, touch me, breathe on me, use me to be a worthy servant of Your Kingdom. Order my steps, order my purpose, set my feet on solid ground, give me what I need to glow in Your light, I just want to serve You, Lord, I just want peace and joy that only You can provide, I want to be happy.

You can do it, Father, You can do it, with You all things are possible, with You I can be the person You always wanted me to be, all power is in Your hands, You are my provider, You are the one and only true living God, there's none greater than You, and I praise, honor, and exalt You. Bless Your holy name, Jesus how sweet the sound, please don't pass me by, I've not done all You asked of me, but Father, I'm trying, believe me, I'm trying.

Your servant

August 9, 2000

Father God,

Thank You for being the God that You are, I praise You to the highest and give You all the glory!

This has been a wonderful day, aside from being my birthday, which I am most grateful for, I've seen on this day answered prayers and I am in awe of Your greatness.

My good friend has evidence of her healing and I just can't thank You enough for that; her cancer has disappeared, Lord, and it's all because of You! I myself had good news in my finance; money appeared that I was not aware of receiving, Lord it's all about You! Another friend testified in church tonight that her test results came back negative, Lord it's all about You! This has been a magnificent day and it's all because of You. You can do all that You say You can do, all our hope comes from You.

I just see Your hand moving in all situations and even if we don't understand Your maneuvers, it always works out on our behalf for fulfillment. Thank You, Lord, thank you, Lord.

You have revealed so much to me, making my understanding clearer and giving me the ability to comfort and encourage others with Your wisdom. I just want to praise and honor You and be the person You want me to be.

As I retire for bed I want to lift up Your name, the name above all names, and thank You for loving me.

SEPTEMBER 10, 2000

On Christ the solid rock I stand all other ground is sinking and, all other ground is sinking sand.

Father, my Savior, my Lord,

I am so filled with love for You and I just want to exalt Your name on high; for there is none greater than You; please forgive me, Lord, for not being all that You want me to be, for not fellowshipping with the saints these last few months the way that I should. I've never eliminated You, Lord, from my life because my spirit is filled with Your presence and I walk in the knowledge of You everywhere I go.

I want more than anything to fulfill the plan You have for my life, I want to be that person, Lord, that You want me to be, I want it so badly, Lord, I just need Your help, I'm trying to do the things that I think will give my life balance, but I'm not so sure I'm doing it right; So, Father, I'm asking You to intervene where necessary, I'm the one You began a great work in and I know You will see it through to completion.

I trust You in every area of my life, and I know You can smooth out all the kinks, You make the impossible; possible, You can use anyone, yes anyone, even me and bring glory to Your Kingdom. I thank You so much for penetrating my heart, for sensitizing it so I can feel the needs and pains of those that need You in their lives, for giving me a few words of encouragement to show interest and concern when needed the most. Thank You, Father, for being my God and giving me a mission here on earth; for showing me what real happiness is, for knowledge, understanding and Your wisdom. You have done great things for me, and I humble myself before You as Your servant and one that has a willing spirit. My heart is true and as long as You walk with me and talk with me and extend Your hand when I fall, I will succeed. I will get Your message out in the way You intend for me to do it.

My peace and my joy all comes from You, use me, Lord, oh Lord please use me.

Your servant

Blessed assurance Jesus is mine! O what a foretaste of glory divine! Heir of salvation, purchase of god, born of his spirit, washed in his blood. This is my story; this is my song, praising my savior all the day long; this is my story; this is my song, praising my savior all the day long.

October 26, 2000

Father God,

Here I am again seeking Your face, because You are master of all, and everything depends on You. I have been trying to make myself happy; I tell myself that gloom or depression will not befall me. I am a child of the King who holds all power in His hands. Father I am still not sure of how to be all that You want me to be.

I am often overwhelmed with financial responsibilities that hold me back from accomplishing my destiny, am I careless with funds, are my priorities out of order, am I not mature enough in these areas, thereby hindering any progress forward?

If this is true I ask You to help me and show me again what I must do and please help me accomplish the goals You have set for me, I can't do anything without Your divine intervention. On my own I am a complete failure, with You by my side I can do all things. Most importantly I want to, in my heart, be a better Christian and walk in Your success.

I am here bringing all my concerns to You, as usual, and Lord, please hear my plea.

I am weary of finding myself at the same point time and time again.

As I study Your Word and seek Your wisdom, reveal to me that which I need to understand, show me the route I need to take and help me to stay on course.

I am weak, but in my weakness I depend on Your strength.

You said You would never leave or forsake me, my confidence in myself is not all it should be, but I have complete confidence in You and what You can do with one even as weak as I .

I have had a tough year, I cried day and night, my heart was hurting so badly and nothing seem to get me back to where I belonged, You saw my tears, You felt my pain and You restored me back to my personality; I greatly appreciate that so much, now I am agonizing over my lack of progress in being a woman of destiny, You've shown me the way yet I can't seem to get there.

I feel as if I'm wasting time, my spirit isn't as high as it should be in many ways, I come, Father, to the only one that can do something; I'm willing and want more than anything to be used in Kingdom building, in whatever way I can, I need from You that which the world can't give, I need Your Holy Ghost power working deep within my soul, I will continue to know You better and maybe one day You will say of me, well done my good and faithful servant.

I thank You for all that You've done thus far, I'm certainly better than I was and You've proven Your faithfulness over and over, because of You I have much to be grateful for and because of You I will never feel alone, with You there is comfort and an answer to all our cares.

Lord, I feel better already.

I pray that all who know You not, will come into the knowledge of Your truth.

January 7, 2001

Father God,

I give You all the honor, I give You all the praise, You are the God of my salvation and I glorify You. I just want to thank You for loving me and giving me new insight every day on Your greatness and Your ability to make changes to activate Your divine plan.

I see You working in my life so magnificently and I am just in awe. Thank You for life, thank You for working out all my concerns, thank You for making the crooked path straight, thank You for answering my prayers, and right before my eyes gave my companion a new vision for his life; for doing for him what You did for me, I see it happening and I sincerely, from the bottom of my heart, thank You. I want to live my life in the good success that was ordained by You.

I see a life before me that will be pleasing to You, I see a life that will help lead others to Your kingdom; I see a future that will be the best and far exceed all that I hoped for. I thank You, Father, I thank You and my faithfulness will never cease.

I will sing praises to Your name, I will be a witness by vision and example, I can be the person You want me to be. I can do all things through You, Lord, You've made me a winner, and I will not forget that fact. The world can be so ugly, but with You there is peace and joy; I've lived so many years in turmoil and grief of one sort or another, but I finally know that life can be different and it all begins with our recognition of You, in trusting You with our lives and not allowing anything to come between our relationship with You. I thank You for giving me a chance to enjoy this reality before it was too late.

I'm on my way to complete happiness and sharing with others this joy.

> Let the heavens and let the earth be glad and let them say among the nations, "The Lord reigns".
>
> (1 Chronicles 16:31)

January 23, 2001

My Father, my Lord, my God,

This year began for me with Your blessing in making my life right in the areas that troubled me the most, and I just want to thank You for answering my prayers and giving me another chance to be the person You want me to be. I want to be an example of all that's good and perfect in Your eyes, I know that in my view I will never be perfect but my view and Yours are not the same, so in my limited understanding I just put my trust in You and try my best to satisfy You in a godly fashion. Give me the wisdom to make the right decisions and to love others more, to control thoughts that are not complimentary to You and focus on things that are good, kind, and lovely.

Help me, Father, to concentrate on carrying out my ministry of encouragement and moving it forward as You would have it in reaching its maximum potential. Expand my mind to higher heights, so that You will be glorified, extend my compassion to its limits and minister to those in need of love and caring. Make my heart sensitive to every emotion that needs attention in even the smallest less visible way and allow me to make some contribution in its recovery if only with a smile, words or just a shoulder to lean on. Direct my path in the direction for this ministry, strengthen my spirit, and help me discipline myself in organizing my time so that I can successfully carry out this mission.

I've made so many promises that I haven't been able to keep, where I am weak, I need Your strength, You've revealed so much to me, but on my own I can't succeed, only with Your help will I be able to accomplished anything. Your word tells me that I can do all things through You, Lord, and I believe that, so here I am, Lord, please use me.

If You use the weak to confront the proud, then here I am, as I am, hiding behind the cross, so that more of You and less of me will be seen, my heart, my soul, my spirit magnify Your name, blessed be the name of the Lord.

Your servant

Lord, all my desire is before You.

(Psalm 38:9)

May 9, 2001

Oh most Heavenly Father, God of the Universe,

I stand humbly before You with praise in my mouth, appreciation, devotion, and love in my heart for You, the most high. Your name reign above all other names and I will never allow anything or anyone to separate my spirit from Yours; I belong to You, we are one.

Please dear Lord, forgive any sin that I may have committed on this day against You, for anything that I may have done or said to anyone that is unkind is as if it were directed intentionally to You personally, and my heart is in pain when I think of grieving You.

I will never be perfect, but Lord, I am trying to be more like You everyday, and I can only be better if I have Your help, so Father, I depend on You.

Thank You for having patience with me, thank You for blessing me in spite of my shortcomings, thank You for answering my payers, and showing me how to live life by Your standards which give the ultimate joy and success; thank You for wisdom and understanding and a happy and humble spirit to share.

On my own I am nothing, with You we are the tag team that wins.

Father, the things of this world weigh heavily on my heart, there is so much going on that is caused by the evil one. I pray that You pour out Your spirit in a big way on those that are held captive. I pray, Lord, for the family of that ten-year-old child that was brutally murdered, please help them, as I know how much they are hurting right now, I too hurt for them. I pray for all those who are living in their own strength without the knowledge of who their God is and that You hold the answer to the world's ills. Only You can fill the void in the lives of those broken, only You can make the crooked paths straight, only You can make the impossible possible, only You can offer life that has meaning, promise, and a hope.

Father, thank You for loving me, for entering my spirit and helping me to realize these things before it was too late, for giving me something to do that will make my life make sense, and for growing me in Your Word a little more everyday, so that I can be a blessing to You and those You bring before me, I pray that I will be to the full extent the person You want me to be and that I don't disappoint You.

I pray to You in the name of the Father, Son, and Holy Spirit.

Amen

Your servant,

Eunice Lewis

September 11, 2001

Father God,

Hear me, please hear me, Lord; today evil came down on our city and thousands of lives were lost because of the hatred in the hearts of man. Oh God! What shall become of us, how do we handle such contempt? It's beyond our scope of understanding. I realize that worldwide people have turned away from You; You have not been taken seriously, there are those who don't acknowledge You at all, and those who belong to the church but only serve You when it's convenient, who are not living according to Your Word or spreading the gospel message. Prayer has been eliminated from schools and the Bible a forbidden subject, pornography rampart and openly accessible on cable and the internet for our children to view; Lustful behavior accepted as the way to go for enjoyment, disrespectful language and dress apparel, our youth existing without a clue about decency and who You are, Lord. This is the time for unity, this is the time for Christians to take a stand, to reflect light in a dark world; this is the time to share Your love to all, this is not the time to just criticize, but to rejoice when a soul is won to You.

This is the time to step out of our comfort zone and talk to others about You, to offer compassion and comfort to those hurting; at this time of excruciating pain is our opportunity to represent that which has been revealed to us in our teaching and exposure, we're aware of the problems, our concentration should be on the solution, and God, I know it begins with love.

Yes it is a love thing, a love that only with Your help can we possess, so that we can effectively answer Your call. Father, I pray for all who think they can have success in this world without You, I pray for all the empty lives that are aimlessly wondering about without hope and so unaware of where hope comes from. I pray that eyes are opened and made aware that You are the answer for the world today, that when we abide in You, and Your word abides in us, we can ask what we desire and it will be done for us, and You will be glorified as we are fruitful, nothing will be impossible for us to achieve, no weapon in hell formed against us will prosper, that a hedge of protection will be around us and we need not fear when we walk through the valley in the shadow of death, because You are with us. We are hard pressed on every side, but not crushed, perplexed, but not abandoned, struck down, but not destroyed (2 Corinthians 4:9).

This disaster has opened many eyes, and we can reap a great harvest for Your Kingdom if we seize the moment, extending kindness at every opportunity, sharing, caring and inviting people to Your church, yes this is the time for the church of God to make our presence known in all areas.

Everyone has a roll, even if it's just by example of the life we're living, and the way we speak to others. This is our time, and Lord, I ask to please help me to be all that

You want me to be, so that I can do my part in whatever way You decide.

Let us not continue to hold past sins of others to remain in our minds, but be willing to joyfully accept their repentance and exercise forgiveness, the same way, Lord, You forgave us.

We're all guilty of something, but Lord, the time has come for hearts and lives to be changed. It's revival time right here in New York City as well as around the world. We can be all that You desire, Lord, because You are our confidence, and if You are for us, who can be against us? You strengthen us, for the gifts and calling You are irrevocable, Your Word is living and powerful, You are our refuge and a present help in trouble, we will not fear, even though the earth be removed, and though the mountains be carried into the midst of the sea, though its waters roar and be troubled, though the mountains shake with its swelling (Psalm 46:1, 3).

You are our God, we are Your people, you will never leave or forsake us, we can rest in Your protection, there is nothing too hard for You, God, You made the heavens and the earth by Your great power and outstretched arm, Through You we will push down our enemies, through Your name we will trample those who rise up against us (Psalm 44:3). Therefore I will look to You, Lord; I will wait for You, the God of my salvation. YOU will hear me, when I fall, I will arise, when I sit in darkness You will be a light to me (Micah 7:7, 8b).

I can rise to the call because You are with me
Blessed be the name of the Lord, who is my anchor.
Here I am, Lord, send me.
Your servant

NOVEMBER 28, 2001

Father God,

I come into Your presence with thanksgiving, glory, and honor to You the one and only true living God. Father, I thank You for all You've done in my life, I don't want You to think for one minute that I've forgotten, or taken lightly Your intervention in my life, how You've heard my prayers and acted on making my crooked path straight, given me a life and a hope for the future. You've answered my prayers with a husband, and manifested Your presence in his life; everyday I see Your hand working on his behalf, making it possible for us to be on one accord. Father I thank You so much for that, because that is the most important thing in my life, I want a mate that recognizes You as the one who holds all power over our lives and makes everything possible for those who sincerely love You. Lord, I want only to be pleasing in Your sight, I want to live my life giving honor to You, I want to be a blessing to others that I come in contact with, even when I'm not aware of it. I don't want the glory for anything You made possible, it all belongs to You. Help me to be a better Christian, help me to absorb more of Your Word so that I can pass it on, help me to act on those things that will fulfill Your will for my life, help me to be more disciplined with finances and health matters, just stay by my side Lord, I need you so much.

Please forgive any sins that I may have committed this day or any previously and didn't realize, I come to You, Lord, seeking to have a clean heart. I pray for the entire world during this very troublesome time, I ask that You enter the hearts of those in decisions making positions so that their actions will reflect a serious concern for people everywhere. I ask that those who have will share with those less fortunate. I pray for revival in this land and there be an outpouring of love for people of all nationalities, because we are one.

I see so much hatred everywhere, even in the church, including the pulpit, and my heart is saddened.

When are people going to get the love message and the extent of its meaning? I know none of us are perfect and the love that's needed to make a difference can only come from serious communion with You, but we have to want it, and be for real about it.

I pray that with all that's happening in the world that Your presence will be sought in a most heartfelt way and healing can take place in all the many areas.

Bless You, Lord, bless my family, friends and all those who are bringing their concerns to You, and enlarge my territory so that I can also be a blessing.

Your humble servant

December 11, 2001

Father God,

I come into your presence with praise, glory, and honor to You the Most High God. You are who You say You are, Lord, I can depend on You, oh You are so wonderful. I love You with my whole heart and You prove over and over again a love so much greater than my mind can conceive.

You have blessed me far beyond measure and I am eternally grateful. I see Your hand in every aspect of my life. I am so glad You have all power in Your hands, what a mess my life would be if it were not for Your intervention.

Right now Lord, I want to thank you for hearing my voice as I asked You to heal my knees from the constant pain I'd been feeling on a daily basis; every step I took, walking up stairs and even as I laid in my bed I was aware of a throbbing pain, and Lord I was reminded in my spirit that You gave me authority over the evil the devil attempts to plague us with "I have given you the power to trample on snakes and scorpions and to defeat the powers of your enemy satan, nothing will harm you." I was reminded that I can lay hands on sickness and expect healing from our Lord and Savior. Father, I did what You gave me authority to do, I laid hands on my knees and rebuked the devil in the name of Jesus and the blood, I demanded that all evil spirits depart from my body and prayed to You, Lord, for healing.

I went to bed and had a restful night, the next day Lord as I was on my way to work I began to realized that I felt no pain in my knees, as I climbed the stairs it was effortless, I began praising and thanking You, Lord, for what You did, I'm healed! I'm healed! And I thank You for healing me. I thank You for Your presence in my life, I thank You for growing me in knowledge and putting those before me who help me in my understanding of Your Word and my inheritance as a child of God. I pray that I will be the person that You want me to be, I pray that I don't disappoint You, I promise that I will constantly strive to be the kind of Christian that will glorify You so that others will know of You, Your saving power and love.

You have never turned Your back on me.

Your servant

> Praise the Lord, O my soul; All my inmost being, praise His holy name, praise the Lord, O my soul, and forget not al His benefits who forgives all your sins and heals all your diseases, who redeems your life from the pit and crowns you with love and compassion, who satisfies your desires with good things so that your youth is renewed like the eagle's.
>
> (Psalm 103)

December 17, 2001

Father God,

It's me here once again coming to You to just honor and adore You. I'm so happy just being in Your kingdom and thinking everyday of all the blessings I've received from You. I can depend on You, Lord, I can dream dreams, I can look to the future with great expectations, I feel vibrant and see my life being fulfilled with hope and desires I had in my youth realized. Only You, Lord could make this possible, only You could give me a talent that would bring attention and glory to You and I'm just so grateful. The void in my life has been filled; I have a song in my heart, and peace through the worst of times, peace that passes all understanding. I am Your workmanship, and the good work that You began will be completed upon Your return, I will live here on earth in victory, because I know who I am in Christ, I know more about You and Your promises to those who love You.

Thank You for being a friend, thank You for loving me, thank You for Your word which strengthens me, and guide me through this world with all it's cruelty, thank You for just being You, God all by yourself.

I don't want to ask for anything right now, I just want to praise You and give reverence to Your holy name.

I worship You, Lord

I worship You; I give honor and glory to You, Lord

I lift my hands up to You for You are the God of my salvation

Hallelujah, hallelujah, hallelujah! Glory to the King of Kings

Oh praise your name, Jesus, Jesus, Jesus

I worship You, Lord; I worship you, Father God Almighty

Glory, glory, glory

Thank You Lord, thank You Father, thank You for saving me

Oh Hallelujah, Hallelujah! Oh praise Your name Jesus, Jesus, Jesus

The Lamb of God

Honor, glory to the Savior of the world.

I love You Lord, I love You.

December 25, 2001

Father God,

Oh bless You, Father, bless You for loving me the way You do, bless You for Your son Jesus Christ, for allowing me to become somebody in Your kingdom. Oh Hallelujah! Hallelujah, Jesus, *joy to the world the Lord is come, let earth receive her King, let every heart prepare Him room...*

Father, I've seen Your hand in every area of my life and I thank You, I thank You for taking over and making the crooked path straight, I thank You for allowing me to finally be able to open my mouth and have words flow out that represent Your presence and bring honor to You. I want to thank You on this your special day of celebration for showing me that my son is under Your care and protection; for just never letting me down and assuring me that You are who You say You are and will do that which You say You will do.

Father, I'm so grateful to You for so much, my heart is so full of love for You and I just want to be pleasing in Your sight. I want to reflect Your love and kindness to others in whatever way You determine; I want to share the gospel and be bold in my witness, I want the world to see how great You are and be an example.

I pray that I'll fulfill my destiny, I pray that You continue to give me necessary wisdom and understanding, I pray that my spirit receive all that is in Your divine plan and that I come to the place that I know what I know and remain humble and sensitive to other people's concerns and pain.

Help me to enlarge my territory and bless me, Lord, so that I can be a blessing.

Lord, everything that I ask is for Your glory, and not mine, if there is any wrong spirit in me I rebuke it in the mighty name of Jesus and stand firm on the authority to use Your name and can expect victory.

Your servant

> But God has chosen the foolish things of the world to put to shame the wise, and God has chosen the weak things of the world to put to shame the things which are mighty.
>
> (1 Corinthians 1:27)

I am weak but in my weakness Father You have shown Your strength...

JANUARY 1, 2002

Father God,

This is the first day of the new year and I want to give thanks to You for allowing me to see this day. I want to thank You for all You've done for me last year and all the years previously. As I reflect on the past my heart is filled with joy as I've recognized Your hand in all that transpired. You gave me a life worth living and hope for the future; my dreams are happening here on earth, You've made the desire of my heart a reality. Oh Lord, I thank You for loving me even when I didn't love myself.

There is so much sorrow in the world and I agonize over all the pain and tears. I want so desperately for love to abound in the hearts of man, I want people of all nations to forget the reasons, forgive and begin to follow the principals in Your Word; the answer is You, Lord, yet so many insist on looking everywhere else in spite of consistent failure.

Lord please use me in whatever way to be a light in this dark world.

Allow this time of suffering to bring about a change, open the eyes of those wandering around in defeat, Oh Father bless this nation and the downtrodden all over the world.

Help me to be a better Christian, help me to extend love and understanding to others in a way that will open the door to Your Kingdom.

You know, Lord, the things that are of the most concern to me, please act on them and guide me in the direction that I should go...

I trust You with my life and know beyond a doubt that You will hear me.

Again I thank You for all that You've done for me and I will be careful to give You all the honor, glory, and praise, for above You there is no other, You are that which You are and in the matchless name of Jesus, I submit all.

Your servant

January 13, 2002

Father God,

It's me again; I come, Lord, I come to You with my heart filled with love and glory to You, the one and only true God. Thank You, Father, for the Holy Spirit and the direction I received to attend a particular church along with my husband because there was a message of importance there on this day for both of us.

I am not always everywhere I should be for growth but, Lord, I try to be as obedient as I can most times and I must say there is always a word for me when I am.

You have given me specific instructions for my future and told me to take the necessary steps and You will bless my efforts; Lord I believe You and now I will move ahead, I will not let the devil tell me I won't succeed. I know who I am, and most important I know who You are and what You are capable of.

I'm stepping out on the faith I have in my heart and the assurance of the truth in Your Word. Yes Lord, it's me, it's me, we know each other, we care for each other, we walk and we talk together day by day, You know my weaknesses and my strengths, but You cover those weaknesses with Your strength and I can't lose with You on my side.

All I have to do is look at what You've already done in my life, how You took control and make the wrongs right for my betterment and Your glory, Oh Lord, it's me and I thank You for this life, I thank You for Your demonstration of love, for opening up my mind to understanding, for allowing me to know you better and developing a relationship that grows more and more everyday; for being the perfect example for me to follow and when I fall short as I go, You continue to pick me up and allow me to start again.

When I need a friend to talk to, there you are, I can come to You with it all and I can be assured of comfort.

There are so many distractions in the world to take ones focus off of you, and Lord, it's not always easy to not indulge in a bit of it, but I know that anything outside of Your order only brings on despair and separation from You and there is nothing worse than that, so I pray that You will always keep me covered with Your hedge of protections and help me to keep my mind stayed on You.

I know that I can do nothing on my own and all that's good and perfect comes from You, Thank You for Your loving-kindness.

Thank You for the message I received in church this morning for both my husband, and myself, I pray that he will know You the same way that I do.

Your servant

January 27, 2002

Father God,

Here I am coming into Your presence with my whole heart overflowing with love and gratitude for the joy that I have that only You can provide. I thank You, Lord, oh how I thank You. You've given me a life I can finally operate in as the person You want me to be. I see a brand new future; I see possibilities today that were far beyond my scope yesterday...

Lord You are who You say You are and You use those whom others see as incompetent, and make them an example of Your greatness, and I bow down to You and bless Your holy name for choosing me, for bringing out talents that I didn't know exist, for giving me words to say of encouragement and a heart to extend love and kindness; Oh thank You, Lord!

Thank You for hearing my cries, for forgiving my sins, for partnering with my spirit and allowing me to be somebody; I look forward to each new day with great expectations, enlarge my territory so that I can bring glory, and honor to you lord, so that all will want to be in relationship with You, because you are the way, the truth and the life.

Open my mind to grater understanding, give me

more of Your wisdom, send me those who are broken and downtrodden, use me to encourage and direct them to your kingdom. Father use me as You please, continue to mold me into the woman that will please you the most.

I pray for my family that You will bless my entire household and give them victory in the areas needed by them individually.

I trust You and know that nothing is impossible for them that love You and are called by Your name.

Not by might but by my spirit says the Lord...

Your servant

MARCH 14, 2002

Father God,

Here I am coming in to Your presence with love, thanksgiving, and praise for all that You have done in my life, I thank You, Lord for giving me the desires of my heart.

I remember not so long ago feeling as if my heart would break, I was so let down with the way my life was going at that time; the one I love so much broke my heart and I though my life was going to be so lonely. I grieved day and night and tried all I knew to put my life back together, nothing worked.

I couldn't bear it any longer so I cried out to You in my pain, bearing all and You heard me. You immediately showed me the way; You intervened and made everything the devil meant for evil, work for good.

I now have a victory story and it's all about You and the love You give, the concern for our happiness, and the lessons You teach.

Oh Father, I have the victory, I have hope, I have a future, right now at this late stage of my life, I have a whole new plan for fulfillment, it comes from You.

I have dreams and they're being realized, I see Your hand in all of it, You've opened my mind to new beginnings. Oh thank You, Lord, thank You so much for loving me.

I will be the person You always wanted me to be, I can do it with Your help, I will never stray away from You, I will never stop in my efforts to know You better, I will trust all Your decisions, no one can do what You do for those who love You.

Thank You for choosing me to help further Your Kingdom, I will do my best.

Your servant

> Behold, happy is the man whom God corrects; therefore do not despise the chastening of the Almighty.
>
> (Job 5:17)

March 29, 2002

> I will bless the Lord at all times; His praises shall continually be in my mouth.
>
> (Psalm 34:1)

Father God,

Today on this Good Friday I am ever so grateful to You for what You did for me, I now have a chance to be the person You want me to be, I commit myself to You just as You committed Your spirit on the cross...

Because of You I see new beginnings being birthed, its real Lord, its real, I've got a dream and its going to be realized because of You, the desires of my heart were resurrected! You brought them to surface and when in my heart I thought it was too late, You showed me that with you there is no such things as too late.

I thank You so much for being active in my life and for connecting in spirit with me, see my heart, Lord, examine it Lord, there is so much love for You there and I just want to be blessing to You. You've been so faithful, you've proven yourself over and over. When I was in my deepest despair You were working it out all along, I saw evil and You came and turned it around, and through it all I was never hungry, never homeless, never naked or jobless. You provided for me and kept me in Your bosom while preparing Your divine plan for my life, Oh Father I can't thank you enough, everything is so much bigger than myself, Your love is so magnificent and I am consumed with Your presence.

I give You my life, I give You my family, I give You all that's connected with me because You hold the world in Your hands and without You there is nothing...

I want to be that person You intended me to be, and I will be that person because I'm committed Father, I'm committed...

Just look at my heart...

April 1, 2002

Heavenly Father,

How excellent is Your name, how sweet the sound, the name above all names, majestic, powerful, glorious, and victorious, Jesus, Jesus, how I love, honor and adore You.

Here I am again in Your presence, seeking to feel the comfort only You can give, seeking to just worship You for a while, seeking to express the deep connection I feel in my spirit for those things that represent You, seeking to be more like You, Lord, seeking to please you in oh so many ways, seeking to spread Your gospel here on earth, Lord open my mouth with words that will glorify You, take charge of my whole self and use me, here I am, here I am, Lord it's me!

Thank you for all Your blessings, thank You for the vision, thank You for showing me that my life is just beginning, I hear Your voice and I know it's You, thank You for filling my heart with joy and for all the revelation knowledge I've received, thank You for Your faithfulness when I didn't deserve it, only You can love that way...

Thank You for entering into my spirit and allowing me to be the person You want me to be, oh I can't thank you enough for that. Thank you for patiently molding me day by day and I will be careful to give You the praise; I close my eyes and meditate on Your goodness and the tears flow in thanksgiving. Thank You for Your wisdom that keeps me from making foolish judgments, or not allowing me to be too proud to ask for forgiveness when convicted by the holy spirit for my wrong doing regardless of how small it might appear to me. Thank you for creating in me a new heart.

Oh Father You are my strength, my healer, my provider, my counselor, my friend, a constant and loyal companion; I can come to You when there's no one else and You'll never let me down, I'm just so grateful to You and I devote my complete being to You. I thank you for new and deeper understanding everyday and I want to share what You've given me with others, please help me do that, yes Lord, enlarge my territory, I'm ready.

Your servant

October 8, 2002

Father God,

It's me Lord, it's me, here I am in Georgia, I've been here three weeks and Father I'm so grateful to You for granting me the desires of my heart, You said You would and You did, oh how I celebrate You for being the God that You are!

I'm so happy and I owe it all to You, I want to make You happy with me, I want You to know my heart so well and I want to be used by You in whatever way You decide, here I am Lord, here I am.

Everyday I awake, I rejoice, Your universe is just so beautiful, there I was in the north thinking how blessed I was to be there and see the wonder of Your creation, I've traveled around parts of the world and I'm just overwhelmed at what I see, there is beauty in every area of the world, how can mankind take it all for granted or just don't appreciate the fullness of it all.

I've been blessed beyond measure, there has been no area of my life that You didn't give meaning and didn't work to make me a better person in Your time; I thank You so much for that, I'm learning and growing everyday, my heart is so full with the desire to be more like You, I want to just be in Your presence, I want to be an example to those who need to know You, to those who have given up, to those who need encouragement, to those who are lonely and need a friend; I want to have something to say to the young as well as the old, I want You to be seen in me in everything I do for Your glory.

I ask that You continue to direct my path, that You place me in the church that You want for me and Your purpose, that the work that You began in me will flourish and love will abound, I'm Yours, Lord, just use me.

There is a plan for me here, enlarge my territory, bless me indeed.

Your servant

October 29, 2002

Father God,

Here I am again, here I am needing to talk with You. I don't know why the enemy is trying so hard to discourage me and attempt to ruin my finances, Lord, I'm not going to let it happen, I'm standing on Your promises, no weapon formed against me will prosper. I belong to the one and only true living God, and I rebuke the enemy in the name of Jesus. Lord, if this is a test, Lord, I'm going to pass it because I know who holds my future.

I know that Your plans are good and perfect and I know that as long as Your spirit is alive and well in my soul that evil can't also be present. I know Father that You will cover me with Your protection, Your Word tells me so, I believe You to be who You say You are and that You will do that which You say You will. I look around me and I see all the wonders of Your kindness, I see all You've done for me and I'm so grateful. I can't thank You enough for Your mercy and grace. I can't thank You enough for accepting me in Your Kingdom, for giving me a chance to be the person You want me to be. Use me Lord, use me, and strengthen me so that I can present Your word to those living in defeat, to encourage those in need of a word from You, use me for Your glory, use me.

God, You put me in this place, You have something specific for me to do here, direct my path, speak to my heart, prepare me for service, without Your strength operating in me I am nothing, Your presence makes the difference, the difference between failing and success.

Lord I just want to serve You and be a part of building Your Kingdom.

Your servant

December 5, 2002

Father God,

I've been indoors all day and my mind has been stayed on You, when I think of the many situations You've brought me through I'm reminded of Your great love and mercy. This is the time of year that I love the most, Lord, because all over the world Your birth is being celebrated. Lord, I just love celebrating You; all the many songs just fill my spirit with reverence and praise.

I look around me and see all the many blessings I've received and I just want to do something that would be pleasing to You in gratitude. Lord I pray that I do those things You want that will glorify You. I want to be used by You, I want to help build Your Kingdom here on earth, I want to extend love and kindness to those who process little hope and tell them Who holds the answer, that with You there is hope and a future. Lord, open my mouth with all the right words to direct the disenchanted in Your direction.

Lord, I pray for direction here in Georgia, guide my path, reveal to me that which You will have me to do, my heart is sincere and filled with Your Spirit, speak to me Lord, speak to me.

Your universe is so beautiful, but man's evil nature

has turned this land into a nightmare, if only we could love the way You loved us, if only man would at least try.

Your word tells us so much; I see the plan You have for us and what a wonderful world there would be if we were obedient to Your principals. Father God if I could help only one person at a time I'd welcome that assignment, I just want to be used by You, to demonstrate Your great power, to be an example, Your example.

Again I say to You, "here I am, use me." Your servant

December 12, 2002

Father God,

This is the day that You have made, I will rejoice and be glad in it. I am so grateful to You when I think of what You've done for me, You are who You say You are and can do what You say You will. I have never been happier than I am now and it's all because of You. You've searched my heart and granted me the desires therein; I owe You so much. You've given me a marriage that is blessed by You, I see Your spirit growing in my husband, he's a new creation, oh how I thank You, Lord. I finally feel like I'm becoming the person You wanted me to be, here I am, Lord, it's me, living the life You provided with all the extras that I always wanted, oh thank You, thank You for being so generous.

I am indeed being blessed and blessed abundantly, what more could I wish for; You've given me everything!

I just want to serve You, serve You in whatever capacity You decide, here I am willing, willing and praying to be a blessing to You, I want the world to know of Your greatness and how You are always there in the time of need, helping with our concerns and giving us comfort and assurance that whatever the situation You will handle it, and that there's no need to worry, every answer we need in any area is found in Your Word. We only have to open our minds to receive and be obedient, even if we don't understand it all, if we just trust You and Your decisions we'll find that it's always the best for us. You are so awesome, Lord, I am so grateful for Your love, so very grateful.

You hear my prayers, I see Your movement throughout my household, You know what's on my heart and You're taking care of all that I ever asked. I don't have to worry about the evil one because You've overcome that threat with Cavalry and the cross, all power is in Your hands and You've given me authority over evil, I'm fully equipped and I thank You for that, I thank You for the sword of the spirit and the victory that it brings.

You are a mighty God the one and only true living God and here I am, your servant.

Lord, establish the works of my hands.

DECEMBER 18, 2002

Father God,

Here I am, again wanting to talk with You and also asking for direction. First I give You honor, glory, and magnify Your name, Jesus as the one and only true living God, maker of heaven and earth, the one who holds all power in his hands. I am so grateful to You for Your love and faithfulness, I can come to You at any hour and You are always there for me, I can expect to receive peace and comfort and assurance that my concerns will be handled by You with my best interest in mind.

My concern is that I don't see the compassion for others in a close family member who is a Christian and operating in the spirit that I feel is required according to Your Word; am I being wrongly judgmental, are there things I don't see, should I just ignore the feeling I feel inside concerning some of the seemingly unkind statements I hear from this person, or should I respond? Father God ,You know the person and the situation, how should I react?

I am not perfect in my own actions, I ask You to help me to be a better person, and to do the things You would have me to do. I don't want to falsely accuse others, I want to be a help, I sincerely want to be pleasing to You and be instrumental in Kingdom building, please direct my path at this point, I am in a new environment, there's a lot to be done here, I just need direction from You. Day by day I wait as I attempt to in some small way be a blessing, some days are better than others yet I know You have something more for me to do.

I will keep You ever present in my heart and continue to strive for excellence as Your servant.

December 24, 2002

Father God,

Here it is, Christmas Eve, just the day before people all over the world celebrate the birth of Jesus Christ our Lord and Savoir. I celebrate you, Lord, everyday, but I also look forward to this day we've set aside to give ourselves a special time to reflect on the birth of Your only begotten Son. I just love this celebration, I just love giving You additional honor, glory, and praise; my heart is so filled with gratitude. Lord I must say that as happy as I am about this time of year, I am also saddened when I think of all those who are not feeling the same as I, those who are heavy burdened, those who have lost loved ones and just can't be happy right now, those who don't know You personally.

Father, I feel compassion for all those who are lonely, for those in nursing homes and feel deserted, those who feel they've lived too long and are no longer useful, those who are looking in all the wrong places for fulfillment, those incarcerated and striped of their manhood/womanhood, those the world keep knocking down and forcing hopelessness into their spirit, those who are doing the right thing according to what they know yet nothing is happening to make their dreams become a reality, those who are sick and find no relief, those who have never taken the time to study and know Your Word.

Father I want to be useful in spreading the good news, I want to be useful in building Your Kingdom, I want what I feel and know to fill the hearts of all those in need, I can't be totally contented otherwise, use me, Lord, however You decide, please use me.

I pray for the world, I pray that man realize what's important, I pray that Your love abound in the heart of all men.

It is so simple, so simple, why is it so hard for those who need to know conceive of a truth that will surely set one free?

Lord, I don't know all the answers, nor do I need to know, some mysteries belong to You, I just know how You entered my spirit and I became brand new, how I longed to know You better, how I became obsessed with being in Your presence, how wonderful I felt, how I saw Your hand orchestrating every move in correcting my steps, and preparing the path for my future. Yes, how I now saw a future for myself, hope was alive! I prayed for wisdom and I received it, I could talk to You and You heard me! I always felt better and knew that with You on my side all things were possible. I never knew this feeling before I came into the knowledge of You, I feel so special, Your Word says that those that belong to You are a peculiar and set aside people; we are special and those in the world can't understand, we're in the world but not of the world, because of this I can sit among kings and not be intimidated, I know who I am, I can live in victory because I am a conqueror, my success isn't measured by the world's standards, I don't attempt to accomplish anything in my own strength, but instead through You, and You never let me down, all my hope comes from You, I acknowledge You as the one and only true living God and no one can separate me from Your love.

What has happened to me could only be of You, as I couldn't do this myself, without You I am nothing.

With You the possibilities are limitless.

Thank You, Father, for Your presence in my life, and most of all Your love.

How sad for those who don't know this joy that the world can't give.

Again, Lord, I say "here I am, use me."

Jabez Prayer,

> Oh that You would bless me indeed, and enlarge my territory, that Your hand will be with me, and that You would keep me from evil, that I may not cause pain! So God granted him what he requested.
>
> (1 Chronicles 4:10)

God I pray that same prayer to You.

Your servant

MARCH 18, 2003

Father God,

Here I am, it's me, it's me and I need to talk with You, I need to feel the warmth and comfort of Your presence. I am so deeply grateful for Your love and kindness; for all the many wonderful things You've blessed me with.

Because of You I am living in a beautiful place, made possible by You and You alone; I have been truly blessed and I'm just so thankful. I don't take anything for granted, all that's good and perfect comes from You, thank You, Father.

Lord I pray for peace, I pray that lives will not be lost based on evil motives, and that whatever happens justice will prevail, that Your direction will lead in the proper direction, because there are no mistakes when You intervene.

I pray for wisdom and guidance during these days of threatened warfare, give me knowledge and tell me how to pray. I come to You, Lord, because there is much I'm not capable of understanding, or facts I do not know. I trust in You, Lord, and believe that You are in charge. There are times when war is the answer, because of the evil that roams the earth like a hungry lion, but it's all in Your hands, Lord, I don't have to know all that's involved,

I just trust You to direct my steps and give me the right words of prayer.

In my heart I want all that are lost to know You, to find peace in an unfriendly world, a peace that surpasses all understanding, to love those who spitefully use us, and as we walk in the light the world will know we are Your disciples and have the victory because this joy that we have the world can't take away.

Thank You, Lord, for entering my spirit and making my life special, for giving me the confidence to be the person You want me to be, as I strive towards that mark. For never giving up on me when I stumble and fall, but constantly picking me up to start all over again with that same confidant spirit to succeed, knowing all along that I can because of You.

You are who You say You are and I am Your servant; I will honor and reverence You forever.

MARCH 20, 2003

Father God,

I come to You tonight with honor and thanksgiving, thanking You first for being the God that You are and loving me as imperfect as I am. Only You, Lord, can love with a love that's far beyond all understanding. You are the God of my salvation and I am forever grateful to You. I thank You for all that You do to make me a better person and for giving me the desires of my heart; you didn't have to do it, because I have such a long way to go to be the person You want me to be, but You did in spite of myself.

I love You, Lord, oh how I love You.

I ask tonight, Lord, for protection on my home during this night of stormy weather, that no harm come to my husband or I and that we go through this night in peace. I ask that on this evening of declared war between the United States and Iraq that Your will be done and that peace prevail. I pray for all those involved and for their safety. I know, Lord, that whatever happens You are in charge, and that although I don't know all the particulars, You know and I just pray for peace and justice; I know You are the God of justice and whatever has to be done You will have Your way and that's where my trust is, in You and You alone.

Lord, again I ask that You use me in ministry in my new community as You desire for me; show me which way to go, put me in a place that will radiate Your presence and that those I come in contact with will see You in me and want to be in an intimate relationship with You for the upbuilding of Your Kingdom here on earth. Use me, Lord, please use me!

Help me to move forward in the things I should do right now; strengthen me and I bind in the name of Jesus any evil spirit that's attempting to discourage me with fear and incompetence.

I am a conqueror and can do all things through You, Christ who strengthens me, love me and want only the best for me. I just have to look around me and see Your mighty works, You are who You say You are and can do what You say You can do. I have the sword of the spirit right here as my guide, thank You for direction, thank You for protection, thank You for love.

June 24, 2003

Father God,

Here I am, Your servant communicating with You the way I've done so often, however Father I haven't done it this way recently, but as You know I've been talking with You on a daily basis. I just want to express my appreciation to You, oh holy one for Your faithfulness, for giving me the desires of my heart, for allowing me to live a life that I thought was non existent. Lord I dreamt of a married life when I was a young impressionable girl, only to marry too young and instead of the marriage I saw on television during fifties that reflected the "American Dream," You know, good husband, typical kids doing the general things kids do, having fun, no violence involved, and of course that nice little house with the picket fence, Lord was I deceived!

Instead my young marriage was a nightmare; Father I was never the same after that failed and broken marriage, life wasn't what I expected. Father I went about in this life looking in all the wrong places for affection, only to receive temporary satisfaction. Living an adult life was so disappointing, why couldn't people live together happily?

What I sought seemed so simple.

A second marriage proved to be worse than the first, filled with hatred and violence. I thought we could be happy, we seemed to have the things that provided happiness.

Again, what I wanted seemed so simple.

Lord, there were times when I though You also hated me, please forgive me for that period in my life, You were there all the time, only I ignored You. I didn't give You authority over my life, I went elsewhere.

In my heart I was a decent person, I don't know how my life got so turned around, but I'm thankful that You finally got through to me; that I realized that only my dependency on You would be my route to peace and happiness. I felt so good being included in Your Kingdom here on earth. I know I was not walking in perfection, but Lord, I was determined to stay closer to You than anyone or thing. I just wanted to be close to You and depend on You to help me be the person You wanted me to be. Lord, You know my heart so You know how sincere I was and still am about being acceptable in Your sight.

Lord, I saw You making my life right in all areas, You blessed me, Lord, to have a marriage that You put together, a home in the country, the way I dreamed of when I was a young girl, You directed my husband and I to a church where we both could be of use and be taught Your Word and grow; I see Your hand on my husband in a mighty way and Father, I'm just so grateful to You for that. We're both where You want us to be for happiness and for the work of the gospel.

Father God, I want to glorify You, I want to lift up

Your name and be a blessing to You, I want You to be seen in everything I do. I want You to use me in whatever way You decide because I know that whatever You do will be for my best interest.

I will never separate myself from You, Lord, I will carry Your Word in my heart always, I will acknowledge You in all things, I will sing Your praise day and night, You are God, my God and there is no one above You, because of You I now have a life, a hope, and a future.

Lord, I can't thank You enough for all that You've done for me; You were faithful to me when I wasn't to You, You allowed me to learn from all my many experiences and just at the right time in my life You gave me the desires of my heart.

You have blessed me abundantly, You are who You say You are and I must tell somebody, I can't keep it to myself, enlarge my territory, and I will be careful to give You the praise.

Let my light so shine for the world to see how great You are...

Your humble servant

July 31, 2003

> I know thy works, your labor, your patience, and that you cannot bear those who are evil. And you have tested those who say they are apostles and are not, and have found them liars; And you have preserved and have patience, and have labored for my name's sake and have not become weary. Nevertheless I have this against you, that you have left your first love.
>
> (Revelation 2:2, 4)

Oh my Love, my Lord, my Savior,

Here I am, Lord, It's me, it's me, maybe You were not referring to me. However, I want to say, I've never left You. I'm in Your presence everyday, You're in my spirit at all times and I desire that You use me however You wish; I just want You to be glorified so the world will know of Your presence. I confess that I've not communicated with You this way, on paper as much as I once did, but my Father, I continue to love You as much as I did in the beginning of my realized love for You; You are my first love and my passion remains the same.

Forgive me for allowing other activities to interfere with this special devotion of the heart we share doing my quiet time at the end of the evening. Although I end my day talking with You before I close my eyes, it's not the same as when I go deep into my heart and bare my soul.

You have honored my prayer.

> Delight thyself in the Lord and He will grant you the desires of your heart.
>
> (Psalm 37:4)

You've made me so happy, You've given me a husband to love and spend my remaining years with. I asked You to give him the passion to know You and the urgent need to walk in Your ways and, Lord, You did that also. Oh, Father, I'm so grateful to You, we have a life and everyday we are blessed by You, we see it, we feel Your hand in every aspect of our lives and I just want to thank You, because You are who You say You are and can do all that You say You can do. You are our hope and when we diligently seek You in love, we will live in peace, a peace that surpasses all understanding by the world's standard.

In my weakness You are my strength, oh thank You, Jesus, I can be the person You intended me to be and fulfill my divine destiny. In my retirement years I can still dream dreams, and they can be realized, I can enjoy being a woman in all the many ways according to my personality, You've been so generous to me; my life now has a new beginning, You did that, Lord, and it's not because I did so many good things. I think You saw me at Your feet so much, trying so hard to express myself to You and finally surrendering myself completely, recognizing You and only You as my source, You could trust my heart to be true, Lord, and I could begin now to go to the next level; this may or may not be all of it… My love continues to soar higher and higher and I am forever grateful for Your faithfulness to someone who doesn't score high in many areas, but whose heart is bursting over with reverence and love to the one and only true living God and I will always be at your feet the same way I was when You first entered my heart.

You are my love, with You there is no stress, no anxiety, no disappointment, no feeling of hopelessness. You've given me so much more than I deserve.

Help me to be all that You require of me to be pleasing in Your sight.

Your servant

January 5, 2004

Oh my Lord, My Wonderful Savior,

Here I am in the new year and my heart is so full of gratitude for all You've done for me. You've answered my prayers over and above my expectations. In my senior years You've given me the best life I could ever want; I feel like a young girl living happily with her soul mate, Oh thank You, Lord, thank You for showing me that nothing is impossible for You and the rewards You grant to those who faithfully love You.

I pray to You and You hear me, You've never disappointed me and You comfort me when I need the warmth of Your embrace.

I asked You to put the same spirit in my husband that You gave me and Lord You did that, I see Your action everywhere and I'm reminded that You are always there, always there beside me, how I love You, Lord.

There's an urgency in me to be more like You want me to be, to fulfill my destiny, to make more visible the talents You've given me that will surely glorify You, Lord, please help me, please help me.

"Oh that You would bless me indeed, and enlarge my territory, that Your hand would be with me, and that You would keep me from evil, that I may not cause pain!"

Just like You granted Jabez his request, please do the same for me.

Please.

Your servant

January 26, 2004

Father God,

It's me, Lord, needing to talk with You and ask You to help me make the right decisions, to help me have the right attitude concerning others and their particular situations. I want to be helpful and encouraging however, sometimes my reaction isn't as kind as it should be, especially if I think commonsense applied would alleviate many of the problems incurred.

Help me to be more compassionate and demonstrate the love and understanding required in order to represent You better. I don't want to be unkind, I don't want to do those things that are displeasing in Your sight, however, the flesh never fails to show its ugly face and I become its victim.

I pray for forgiveness, I pray that You will remove any bad spirit that is attempting to occupy space in my being, I pray that I will only be a blessing to those in need of Your kindness and that kindness will be seen in me, while glorifying You.

Without Your divine intervention I am nothing and will surely fail in my own strength; I need You.

Oh Lord; bless me this day, please!

I am so miserable when my thoughts become my

enemy. Lord, restore in me a clean heart, I am not perfect, I'm so far from it, help me to live right, help me to think right, and help me to love right.

Lord, You and only You can help me to be the person You want me to be, so here I am Lord, here I am.

Your servant

> Let integrity and uprightness preserve me, for I wait for you.
>
> (Psalm 25:21)

FEBRUARY 15, 2006

Father God,

It's been awhile since I've communicated with You this way, You are always with me and I still continue to communicate with You within the secrecy of my mind. You are the only one that I trust; You've proven Your faithfulness in so many ways. I realize how much I need You more and more each day.

Lord, as You know I've procrastinated on many things, but I continue to be plagued by the fact that I've not made the effort required to put these letters in print in order to share them with others as You directed some time ago.

So Lord, here they are and if they are going to be meaningful to someone it will be because You know more than I on all things. I pray that You will bless this effort and that You continue to help me on this Christian journey.

I will forever be faithful to You and thank You for all the happiness You've given me.

I am living the best life I've ever had and it's all because of You.

I can't praise You enough; I want the world to know.

Please continue to use me for Your purpose.

Your servant